Multimedia for Decision Makers

A Business Primer

Jeff Burger

∴

ADDISON-WESLEY PUBLISHING COMPANY

Reading, Massachusetts   Menlo Park, California

New York   Don Mills, Ontario

Wokingham, England   Amsterdam   Bonn

Sydney   Singapore   Tokyo   Madrid   San Juan

Paris   Seoul   Milan   Mexico City   Taipei

Many of the designations used by manufacturers and sellers to distinguish their products are claimed as trademarks. Where those designations appear in this book, and Addison-Wesley was aware of a trademark claim, the designations have been printed in initial capital letters or all capital letters.

The authors and publishers have taken care in preparation of this book, but make no expressed or implied warranty of any kind and assume no responsibility for errors or omissions. No liability is assumed for incidental or consequential damages in connection with or arising out of the use of the information or programs contained herein.

Library of Congress Cataloging-in-Publication Data

Burger, Jeff.
    Multimedia for decision makers : a business primer / Jeff Burger.
      p. cm.
    Includes index.
    ISBN 0-201-40836-8
    1. Management information systems. 2. Decision support systems. 3. Multimedia systems. 4. Interactive multimedia. I. Title.
    HD30.213.B868 1994
    658.4'038—dc20
                                       94-34625
                                          CIP

Sponsoring Editor: Philip Sutherland
Project Editor: Joanne Clapp Fullagar
Production Coordinator: Debbie McKenna
Front cover art: Jeff Burger
Cover art source photos © Copyright 1993 Photodisc, Inc.
Illustrations: Vickie Rinehart
Technical editing: Phil Hood

Set in 11 point Bembo by Jacqueline Davies.

Addison-Wesley books are available for bulk purchases by corporations, institutions, and other organizations. For more information please contact the Corporate, Government, and Special Sales Department at (800) 238-9682.

1 2 3 4 5 6 7 8 9-MA-9998979695
First printing, November 1994

Acknowledgments

This book is dedicated to the growing multimedia industry, to all my friends and family, and to my extended family at *NewMedia* magazine

Special thanks to Phil Hood at *NewMedia* for an excellent technical edit

Special thanks to Vickie Rinehart for the great graphics and years of encouragement

Table of Contents

5.
Audio Tools

6.
Video Tools

7.
Media Integration and Delivery

8.
Investment Decisions and Preliminaries

9.
The Production Process

10.
Business Presentations

11.
Major Productions

12.
Training

13.
Reaching the Consumer

14.
Information Management

15.
Business Communications

16.
Future Directions

Introduction: Hype or Reality?

The term "multimedia" is perhaps one of the most widely used and abused buzzwords in recent years. As recently as 1990, the first incarnations were born more of marketing hype than of technology. Much of the true promise of multimedia was merely "smoke and mirrors" at the time, and many other manufacturers stretched the vague definitions to associate the label with just about anything imaginable.

Multimedia debuted with a great deal of hype

Since then, however, multimedia technology has matured at an astounding rate. It is unquestionably the hottest area of the computing industry, both in capability and technology advances. Today's computers and related multimedia tools are truly redefining the nature of computing, communication, education, and entertainment. It is also affecting other traditional media industries such as publishing, audio, video, graphics, and more. Smoke and mirrors have largely been replaced by new paradigms for interactive audio-visual experiences or information that in many ways represents the culmination of all communicative arts to date. In short, multimedia is very much real.

Multimedia has matured into a powerful communication tool

Multimedia has undergone many of the growing pains experienced by other media at their inception. Desktop publishing provides perhaps the most recent example. Manufacturers fostered the notion that everyone can and will create sophisticated layouts on their desktops by simply buying a few snazzy pieces of hardware and software. The reality is that quality results require design skills and an understanding of technology best delegated to specialists.

The evolution is much like that of desktop publishing

Multimedia amplifies the desktop publishing scenario by potentially mixing the technology and disciplines of text, graphics, animation, speech, music, video, interactivity, computer programming, and more. Few individuals possess all of these skills, leading to the conclusion that the best multimedia productions are often team efforts. It also leads to the conclusion that (with the possible exception of basic presentations) multimedia is a responsibility to be delegated by management. Few managers or business

Multimedia is now often delegated to specialists

professionals would consider the actual multimedia production process to be an effective use of their time even if they possess the interest and skills.

The multimedia market is expanding

Another growing pain is the transition from generics to vertical markets. The first wave of information in any new medium—print, radio, film, television, or computers—has typically been about the related technology, tools, and techniques. As the training wheels come off, the market for applications of the media expand. In print we have genres such as fiction and nonfiction, subdivided into categories such as fantasy, romance, suspense, mystery, sci-fi, reference, travel, and so forth. Television offers a wide palette including news, topical magazines, soap operas, sitcoms, talk shows, and drama. And in computing we have areas of specialization such as business productivity, scientific, media production, and games.

Business is the most widespread market for multimedia

Multimedia has now matured to the point where discussions of technology and skills are only of real use to individuals actually fulfilling projects. The time has come to address vertical markets. Multimedia can be divided into three major categories—business, education, and consumer. The latter is just beginning to come of age and will largely revolve around experiencing content that is created elsewhere. Education is embracing multimedia as best it can on limited budgets. Business, in all of its incarnations, is the hotbed of multimedia activity today. Business always has a message to communicate to prospects, customers, employees, and trading partners—and multimedia is simply the latest, greatest communication tool.

This book is an overview for business decision makers

The book you hold in your hands is designed to be a sister publication to *The Desktop Multimedia Bible*. The goal of *The Desktop Multimedia Bible* is to provide a detailed reference for those who indeed wish to get their fingernails dirty creating multimedia of all kinds and is not specific to any one area of application. While I am pleased that it has become one of the most highly acclaimed works on the subject, multimedia has evolved to the point where many managers, business professionals, and other decisions makers need a perspective on multimedia from a higher level—and one oriented to the business world. You need an understanding of what multimedia means to your business communication efforts. You need perspectives on its uses in presentations, trade shows, training, retail, and direct marketing. You need to know how much it costs, how to invest in equipment, and how to hire or contract the necessary human resources. This book is for you.

1

Defining Multimedia

One of multimedia's growing pains has been the lack of a universal definition. Multimedia has different meanings to different people and businesses. The most common definition is the merging of graphics, text, sound, and video in various combinations with the computer and with which the user can often interact. (The category of graphics includes art, photos, and animation; sound includes music, speech, and sound effects.) The most powerful vision is the marriage of television's communicative powers with the information storage and access abilities of the computer (see Figure 1.1).

Multimedia is the integration of graphics, text, sound, and video with computers

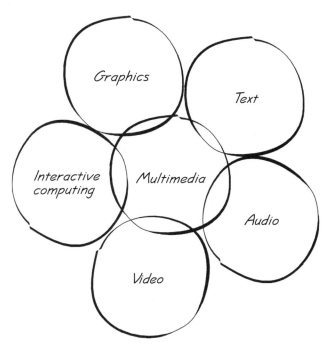

FIGURE 1.1 Multimedia is media integration.

Perhaps the most powerful statement made in my book, *The Desktop Multimedia Bible*, is that "multimedia is not about technology, but about effective communication." The best way to understand the genre as a whole is to examine it from a variety of perspectives and criteria including media, people, applications, and orientation.

Effective communication is the most important criteria

Evolution or Revolution?

Multimedia began as computer control of traditional media

At first glance, multimedia may appear to be a revolution that occurred almost overnight. In actuality, it represents the evolution and synergistic integration of digital technology with various media. The important part of the story began with the popularization of low-cost desktop computers in the early 1980s. While largely used for business tasks such as databases, spreadsheets, word processing, and accounting, the computer also became a controller for traditional analog media devices such as printers, slide projectors, video editors, and music synthesizers.

Most media have evolved into digital form over the last decade

As technology advanced, many of these devices became digital in nature—essentially dedicated computers. By the second half of the 1980s, the graphic and print industries were revolutionized by desktop design and publishing. The video industry was partially transformed by desktop video and graphics, as well as the popularization of consumer VCRs and camcorders. And the music industry was turned on its ear by personal and project studios using MIDI and desktop audio.

Computers now play respectable graphics and sound

In tandem, personal computers and related components such as processors, memory, and storage followed the oft-cited formula of "twice the power at half the price every two years." Given the proper software and input and output devices, the computers on our desks became capable of handling many of the tasks previously relegated to dedicated media tools. Medium- to high-resolution graphics became a given, and many users embraced internal sound (largely as a result of the game market). Overlaying graphics on an external video signal became inexpensive. And software tools for integrating and navigating these media components became more refined (see Figure 1.2).

FIGURE 1.2 Evolution of multimedia

Computer control — Early '80s → Digital media — Mid to late '80s → Computer integration of digital media — Early '90s

Computer-based digital video completed the equation

As the most demanding medium—video—recently began finding its way directly into the computer, the final barriers to comprehensive media integration began to crumble. Further enabled by standards, smaller com-

2

ponents, and the mass storage capabilities of today's hard drives and CD-ROMs, multimedia is today a practical tool.

Benefits of Multimedia

At first glance, the primary benefit of multimedia is the combination of several traditional media. Text offers clarity and self-pacing. The spoken word can be even more accessible. Graphics provide visualization and communicate style. Music imparts mood and character. Video captures the moving events of the world around us. Computers store and access vast amounts of information. Various combinations of these media and disciplines can indeed be formidable communication vehicles: Speakers are more effective, learning takes place more quickly, group consensus are easier to reach, and ideas are communicated more clearly and completely.

Multimedia draws from component media

Most of the additional benefits of multimedia stem from the digital nature of most related media. Digital information suffers no generation loss when replicated or transmitted. Back-up copies of media are simple to create. Manipulation and editing can be performed without altering the original. Powerful manipulation once requiring expensive hardware can be performed with software alone on digital content. Repetitious production tasks can be automated. And massive amounts of content can be easily stored and distributed on inexpensive media such as CD-ROMs.

Digital media in general have many benefits

Digital media also typically implies random access. Linear media such as videotapes and books can only be searched and navigated indirectly and tediously. When segments are properly indexed or linked, random access allows one to jump to any point in the media almost instantly—beneficial in both the production and viewing processes. During the process of editing a video stored on hard disk, for example, a tremendous amount of creative time can be saved by instantaneous location of any point in the program.

Random access is an attribute of most digital media

One of the most powerful assets of multimedia—interactivity—is essentially random access in the hands of the presenter or viewer. Interactivity in a presentation, for example, provides the ability to instantly review points in response to audience questions. In training, it repeats and coaches in areas of difficulty during testing. In productions such as electronic cata-

Random access paves the way to interaction

logs, interactivity allows the user to directly access the exact information desired. Studies have shown that information is better retained in some modes compared to others: 20 percent by hearing, 40 percent by seeing, and 80 percent by doing. Interactivity brings a vehicle for "doing" to otherwise passive media.

Digital information can be stored and transmitted with little regard for content

Finally, digitization of information in any form is a great equalizer. Once information becomes a stream of ones and zeros, the only distinction between audio, video, graphics, text, and programs lies in each one's volume and interpretation. This allows a single medium such as CD-ROM or hard disk to hold all of these data types. It also allows standard communication pathways such as local-area networks and telephone lines to transmit them without regard for content or form.

The Human Factor

Multimedia can be equally defined by human involvement

The people involved with multimedia can be categorized according to those who create it and those who experience it. In this respect it parallels other media. Movie studios make films for audiences to view, just as publishers create magazines, newspapers, and books for mass consumption.

Powerful media technology is now accessible to anyone with a message

As technology becomes ubiquitous, cheaper, and more powerful, however, it becomes more accessible to those who have a need or desire to express themselves creatively in media. Camcorders and inexpensive editing equipment are one example of the "prosumer" phenomenon where decent-quality creative tools are accessible to anyone with a moderate budget. Similarly, desktop publishing brought the power of the design studio and printing press to the average business—incredible progress from the days when even the technology of handwriting was largely restricted to religious scribes.

Most ambitious multimedia projects require teamwork

Multimedia technology does make incredible communication power available at prices accessible to most individuals and companies. Perhaps the greatest myth surrounding multimedia is that the average individual will create multimedia single-handedly. The message trumpeted by many manufacturers is that the mere purchase of their products will turn you into a desktop Spielberg. In reality, technology is not a substitute for talent. While many basic business presentations are created by individuals, more ambitious projects typically require the skills of many individuals.

The Triangle: Converging Skills

The three major orientations or mindsets essential to successful multimedia projects of any scope are creative, technical, and business. Creative talent is necessary in order to make the message compelling. Technical skills (or the willingness to develop them) are required in order to transform creative desires into reality. And business savvy is necessary to ensure that the message hits its mark while the production budget remains fluid. Many people have a combination of two or three of these orientations. Envision a triangle with creativity, technology, and business at the three corners. You should be able to place yourself at a point within this space that represents your balance of mindsets. This same model is also helpful in visualizing the talents of others (see Figure 1.3).

Creativity, technology, and business skills are production requisites

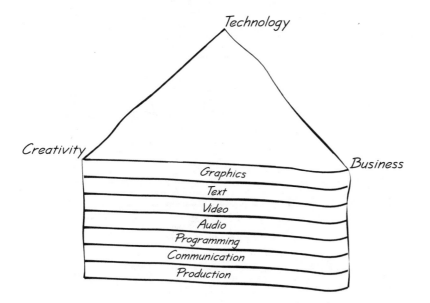

FIGURE 1.3
The triangle of creative, technology, and business orientation

The triangle model is an extension of the left-brain, right-brain qualities we encounter in life in general. Multimedia adds various strata that represent media and disciplines. Depending upon the project, those strata can include graphics, text, audio, video, computing, marketing, and overall production. Adding these strata to the triangle model makes it possible to position one's disciplinary attributes as multiple points within this space. It also serves as an excellent model in which to evaluate the attributes of others in terms of team needs for a given project (see Figure 1.3).

Those orientations extend to media disciplines

An examination of the credits at the end of a motion picture reveals the many specialized disciplines that must intermesh to yield a compelling production. Multimedia productions can be anywhere from simple to complex. The closer a production needs to be to the aesthetics of Hollywood and Madison Avenue, the more talent is required. There are certainly a handful of Renaissance people who are equally adept at multiple disciplines. These individuals typically make the best multimedia producers and visionaries. On sophisticated projects they, in turn, hire the talents of team members to fulfill the various pieces of the media puzzle—partially because the time constraints often demand parallel production tasks.

FIGURE 1.4
Basic timeline of an average production

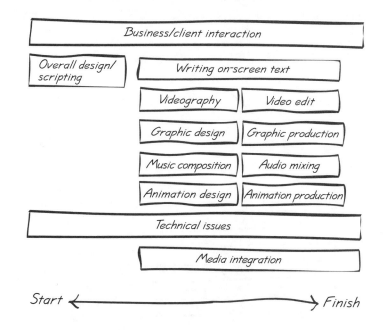

The Web: Converging Industries

Another problem people often have in defining multimedia is in the very act itself. The implication is that multimedia is a finite thing that ought to be nailed down. By extension, multimedia is often perceived as being distinct from traditional media and something that people jump to rather than evolve into. "I want to get into multimedia" is a commonly heard phrase. In actuality, it is more of a two-way street. Multimedia does not replace or obviate traditional disciplines and media. Industries such as graphics, photography, publishing, music, video, computing, and consumer electronics have contributed to the multimedia melting pot through their technological advances. Skills from these industries are also necessary in the production of quality multimedia. In this sense, multimedia is a hub with two-way arteries to other industries (see Figure 1.5).

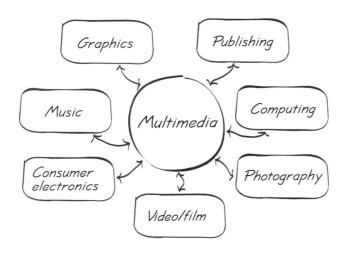

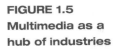

FIGURE 1.5
Multimedia as a
hub of industries

Looking at it another way, digital technologies are causing various media industries to borrow from and fuse with one another. As an example, photographers can now easily archive their images digitally on CD-ROM using Kodak's Photo CD technology. This same technology allows audio for music and narration to be placed on the same disk and provides for the structuring of interactive navigation paths to allow user-control of the viewing experience. An equally valid depiction of multimedia might then be that of a web in which multiple industries are interconnected (see Figure 1.6).

Multimedia merges traditional media industries

**FIGURE 1.6
Multimedia as a
web of industries**

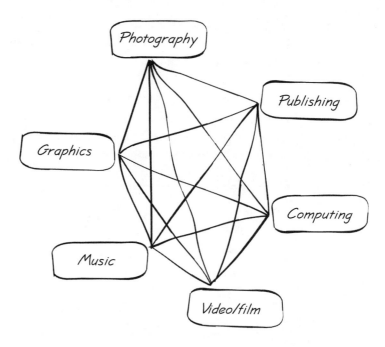

Real-World Applications

*Multimedia is best
described by its use*

The ultimate method of defining multimedia is by its application. We
rarely describe video, for example, as the integration of moving imagery
and sound. Instead, it is described in context—industrial, educational,
entertainment, and so forth. The major categories for multimedia are
business, government, education, entertainment, and communication.
Each has its subset categories, as well (see Figure 1.7).

**FIGURE 1.7
Basic multimedia
application
categories**

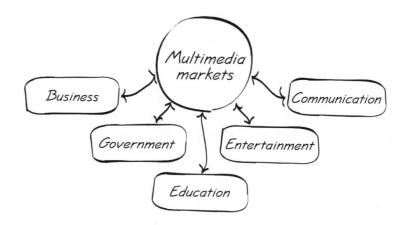

Business

Business is a logical mainstream market for multimedia. Virtually all businesses have the need to communicate. The nature of that communication varies from business to business. Communication has traditionally been done verbally, in person, in print, with slide shows, and on video. Multimedia has the ability to emulate each of these standard vehicles, as well as combine them in powerful ways. Applications include sales/marketing presentations, trade-show productions, employee training, direct marketing, retail vending, and point-of-sale information. In depth examination of these uses constitute most of the remainder of this book (see Figure 1.8).

Businesses are reaping the greatest benefit of new media

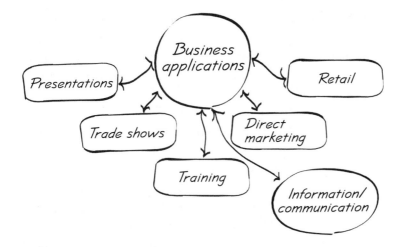

FIGURE 1.8 **Business applications for multimedia**

Government

Government, in the form of the military, is one of the earliest adopters of multimedia technology. Laserdisc players under computer control have been used for various forms of military training almost since the inception of that medium. Similarly, CD-ROMs have been used for electronic documentation such as the massive service manuals for nuclear submarines. Laptop computers outfitted for cellular communication were instrumental in the Persian Gulf war. As these and other technologies converge, the military is likely to continue pushing multimedia to its limits.

The military was the first to embrace multimedia

Multimedia and related technologies can also aid traditional government branches in the massive load of administrative tasks and one-to-many interaction. Kiosks incorporating graphics, sound, modems, and vending act as electronic agents for many state lotteries. The State of California is also in the process of installing kiosks all over the state that will accept payment for traffic tickets and renew drivers' licenses. While this book focuses on business applications, many potential uses of this technology in government closely parallel those of nongovernment industries.

Education

Interactive audio-visual content is a powerful educational tool

Education is an extremely powerful application for multimedia. The value of supplementing dry textbooks with film and video has been recognized for years. Multimedia not only offers the ability to integrate this same audio-visual experience directly with text, but adds the power of interactivity. Students can learn at their own pace. They can be automatically tested for comprehension at strategic points and seamlessly taken back through remedial lessons when unacceptable results are detected. Interactivity allows the curious to easily take side trips to explore related topics and concepts. Students can even assemble audio-visual reports from various media relating to a homework topic (learning something about communication and production along the way).

Interactivity personalizes the learning process for students

Reference materials can take on added dimension and effectiveness when imbued with technology. Let's say a child is learning about lions. A multimedia encyclopedia can present much more than a static image and dry text. For starters, video clips can bring the sights and sounds of lions in the wild to the screen. Options might be presented for subtopics such as habitat, predators, food, and so forth. Exploration of the food subtopic might reveal that lions are predators of gazelles. Information about gazelles would ideally be linked so that it is only a mouse-click away (see Figure 1.9). One could then see gazelles in the wild and explore their habitat, population, and food.

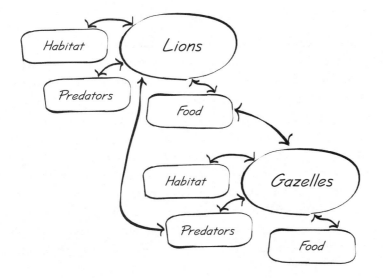

FIGURE 1.9
Basic model for interactive reference materials

Multimedia brings new paradigms to education. The term "edutainment" has been coined to describe the embodiment of educational content in entertainment genres that appeal to a generation raised on video games, arcades, and music television. Learning about Leonardo da Vinci, for example, would be much more compelling if a student could meet a virtual Leonardo on the screen and explore various projects in his studio with him. Similarly, learning about space travel could be very exciting if students were allowed to pilot a space shuttle simulator on screen. The transformation of information into a game or music video can make virtually any subject more compelling.

"Edutainment" represents a new educational paradigm

Even preschoolers are given a head start through interactive storybooks and virtual playgrounds that promote exploration while teaching fundamentals such as morals, language, and association. Such titles can mesmerize children for hours with much more meaningful results than simple storytelling or TV viewing. The bad news is that funding for public schools and associated technology is in crisis. The good news is that educational multimedia titles allow parents to supplement their children's learning process at home.

Multimedia extends education into the home

Consumer Market

The consumer market will ultimately be the largest market

Edutainment crosses the line between education and entertainment. Home entertainment and the consumer market in general represent the Holy Grail of multimedia. In addition to edutainment, applications include video-on-demand, music-on-demand, games, reference tools, interactive fiction, home shopping, and more. The vehicles for home entertainment include personal computers, set-top CD-ROM players, and services provided via cable and telephone connections (see Figure 1.10). This market is now seeing meaningful movement, with some computer game titles selling over one million copies. An important distinction is that the emphasis in this market is on users as consumers of content, rather than on producers. The range of possible applications and delivery vehicles is discussed in greater detail in Chapter 16, "Future Directions."

FIGURE 1.10
Some consumer applications of multimedia

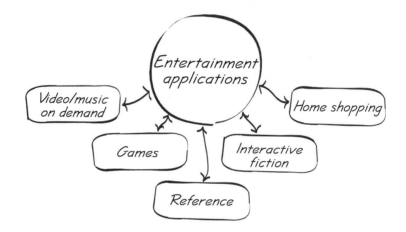

Communication

Integration will extend the impact of new media

Until quite recently, multimedia has primarily been confined to dedicated hardware, and titles are usually developed to play on specific platforms. Multimedia and communication technologies are plummeting inevitably toward one another. Their integration impacts the areas of business, education, and entertainment equally and significantly.

Multimedia provides a universal pathway for communication

As mentioned earlier, multimedia content primarily takes the form of digital data. Local-area and wide-area networks communicate digital data, as does the new generation of telephone and cable systems. Over the next decade, speed and standards issues will disappear. Businesses will reap the benefits of V-mail (video mail), desktop videoconferencing and networked multimedia. Education in businesses, schools, and homes will be empowered by distance learning and "telepresence." Two-way audio-visual connection with and interactive navigation of the "global village" will revolutionize home entertainment, everyday communication, and potentially even the democratic process (see Figure 1.11). The impact of the integration of communication and multimedia technologies is discussed in Chapter 16, "Future Directions."

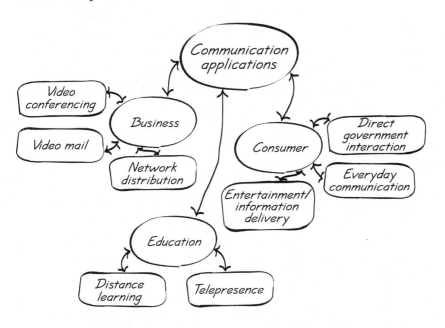

FIGURE 1.11
Some communication applications of multimedia

Other Classification Perspectives

We've taken a quick look at ways in which multimedia can be defined according to technology, benefits, people, and real-world applications. Here are few more ways in which it may be evaluated.

More criteria to categorize multimedia

Orientation: Passive vs. Interactive

While one of the most powerful and intriguing attributes of multimedia is the potential for interactivity, there's nothing that says a desktop production has to be interactive. A passive production—one that unfolds linearly every time—can be created with the same tool set and media combinations as an interactive production. A videotape is an example of a linear,

Content can be either passive or interactive

passively viewed production. Video is still a practical medium for mass distribution, and desktop technology has significantly lowered video production budgets while making possible effects previously available only in high-end studios.

There are many levels of interactivity

Interactivity can take many forms, loosely grouped into linear and non-linear. The simplest linear example is the click-to-advance model descended from the slide show. Bank ATMs are an example of guided interactivity through a linear process. Simple non-linear interactivity employs point-of-interest departures from an otherwise passive production—personal explorations that supplement the main track of the content. Educational and training models typically break a structured presentation into bite-sized chunks of information and interactively test for comprehension at the end of each. Titles that provide free-form exploration of a topic require a great deal of user interaction. And games represent a genre where nothing typically happens at all without human intervention.

Interactive control devices take various forms

With interactivity comes the choice of control devices. Few content designers rely on the computer keyboard for anything beyond expert-level functions. The mouse is the de facto standard for mass-distributed titles. Consumer electronics manufacturers are embracing something more resembling video game controllers. Touchscreens are often the most practical for kiosks and their exposure to the elements and multiple users. Regardless of the physical mechanism, intuitive and attractive interface design is one of the new art forms emerging from multimedia.

Systems: Production versus Delivery

System requirements differ for delivery and production

As with other media, the demands on production and delivery systems are not always the same (see Figure 1.12). The delivery system needs to accept or incorporate the final distribution medium, as well as have the associated hardware required to play back any incorporated elements such as graphics, audio, and video. Beyond that the system must have enough speed and fidelity to play back the content at reasonable quality.

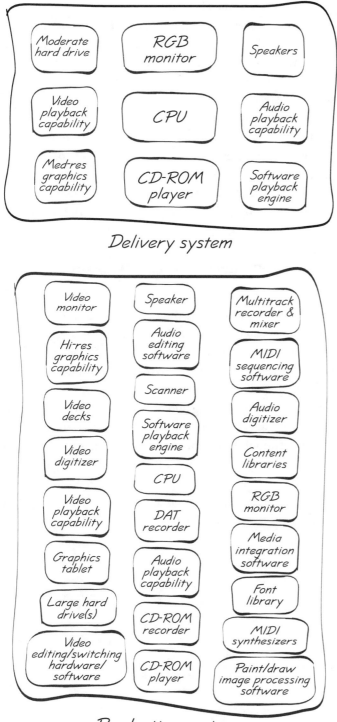

Delivery system

Production system

FIGURE 1.12
Delivery versus production system requirements

Production systems require more hardware and software tools

The production system(s) must have the same capabilities as the delivery system, as well as the software and hardware tools to create the content. Whereas the average delivery system doesn't need to have audio and video digitizing hardware, for example, the production system must have it if the production process includes acquiring those elements from nondigital source material. Video decks, video switchers, cameras, scanners, musical instruments, multitrack recorders, and graphics tablets are other examples of hardware that may be required during production. Production software needs might include applications for authoring, image processing, painting/drawing, sound editing, MIDI recording, and content libraries. The exact complement of hardware and software required varies depending upon the nature of the project. Production and delivery tools are discussed further in the next few chapters.

Self-Contained versus Peripherals

The trend is toward complete computer integration

In the early days of multimedia, the computer typically only had enough power to control other devices. Training environments, for example, would often combine a computer with a laserdisc player. The selection and testing process would take the form of text and simple graphics on the computer which would, in turn, control the laserdisc player to present appropriate linear segments of lessons on video. Today's technological advances are rapidly incorporating audio and video playback capabilities into the computer, either natively or through the addition of cards to the expansion buses. Though this is the desirable and logical trend, there's no rule that says multimedia delivery must be completely self-contained within the computer. The latest generation of multimedia computers even incorporates microphones and cameras aimed at video mail and other business applications (see Figure 1.13).

FIGURE 1.13
Peripheral options

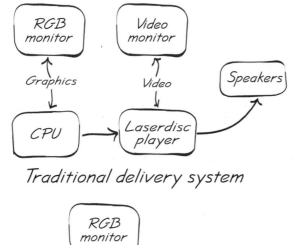

Traditional delivery system

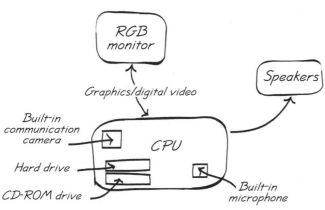

Modern delivery/desktop system

Industry Orientation

Yet another way to look at multimedia is industry orientation. In the big picture, the multimedia computing industry is attempting to rival Hollywood and Madison Avenue. Some observers see this as the logical evolution of computer-based technology. Others have claimed it to be an attempt on the part of the computer industry to perpetuate the ongoing need for more hardware, software, and processing power so that we continue to purchase new tools. Both perspectives are probably valid!

Multimedia is both logical evolution and industry hype

Messages of empowerment are best tempered with reality

The real danger is that the computer industry is known for selling boxes in a manner outdone only by the legendary car salesman. What the public is being sold is largely the potential of empowerment. Five years ago there was little desire on the part of end-users to combine so many media with the computer—the manufacturers just put it out there along with the promise of the big, bright future. The public is now excited about the potential, but isn't necessarily clear on how to use the tools for the promised results. By contrast, Hollywood and Madison Avenue have a track record of placing creativity over technology. The simple caveat here is that it is wise to take the messages coming from multimedia manufacturers with a grain of salt.

Originality

Initially, multimedia poorly emulated existing genres

While this criteria applies more to consumer-level titles than business, it is nonetheless worth mentioning. History has shown that new media in their formative years emulated existing media before taking on a unique form of their own; for example, radio borrowed from books and magazines in the heyday of the serial. Similarly, television in the 1950s largely emulated the stage with variety and game shows before growing to its present level of diversity. True to form, the first multimedia offerings largely rehashed existing material ranging from board games to arcades to reference materials. Much of this was done so poorly in the opening rounds that it gave multimedia a bad name.

Multimedia should be judged by its effective use of the medium

Multimedia is slowly coming into its own. Forward thinkers are using the technology to create compelling content that truly represents a new paradigm in media experience. The true test of a multimedia production, however, lies not with its originality, but with its effective use of the medium. We must embrace only the electronic books that bring a richer experience than the print version and chastise those that do not. We must patronize content providers that give us new ways to access and cross-reference the knowledge of mankind and forsake those who merely throw a slew of public domain images on a CD and call it multimedia. And in the production of multimedia, we must ask ourselves if we're using the media to its fullest potential.

Media Integration

Coming full circle, we've established that multimedia has the potential to integrate graphics, text, audio, video, and interactivity. In dispelling any remaining myths about what multimedia is and isn't, it is important to emphasize that not all of these media need be present in order for a production to qualify as multimedia. Television might arguably be called multimedia because it integrates moving imagery, sound, and communication technologies. Before the popularization of computers, multi-image slide shows with soundtracks were also called multimedia.

Multimedia can include media elements in various mixtures

Creatively, someone skilled in one medium may wish to add the elements of one or more other media. An artist may, for example, wish to add music to a portfolio of images that are distributed on CD-ROM. Some would call that multimedia, others would simply say that it's a CD with art and music. Ultimately, the distinction is not important—the effectiveness of the end results are!

Effective results should take priority over definitions

So much hype and poor definitions have surrounded this subject that the best way to clarify multimedia is ultimately to move beyond the term altogether. We are simply in an age in which the synergy of digital media is becoming a way of life. Certainly the power to integrate these various media with the ubiquitous computer empowers us with communication potential unprecedented in human history. Certainly, we'll continue to refer to multimedia throughout this book, but the choices of media elements, personnel, scope, and message are ultimately so diverse yet project-specific that it is more practical to think in terms of applying computer-based digital media to our business needs.

Multimedia is ultimately the application of digital media to projects

2

Technology Overview

The goal of this book is to provide perspectives on real-world applications of multimedia without getting caught up in technology. An understanding of some fundamental technical concepts, however, will nonetheless be extremely useful in understanding strengths, weaknesses, potential, and limitations as you make decisions about putting new media to work for you. We'll stay away from rocket science and finite details, instead examining issues that bear on the practical application of multimedia on the whole.

A technical overview will put issues in perspective

All too often the definition of multimedia as the marriage of conventional media with the computer is taken literally. While the computer may rightly be regarded as being capable of tasks related to any of these media, there are issues of efficiency—both in the individual disciplines and their successful union. Traditional audio and video in particular rely heavily on standards and strict tolerances with regard to signal parameters, timing, physical media, and playback devices. Transforming the generic computer into an interactive audio-visual machine brings issues relating to all of these factors.

Multimedia computing addresses issues of its component media

Two Worlds: Digital versus Analog

The natural world we live in is *analog*, which can be defined as continuous flow capable of fluctuation. Water currents, wind, landscape, and even the flow of blood in our veins are all analog—as are human senses such as sound and vision. Electricity, magnetism, and the radio frequencies used to broadcast television, radio, and cellular phones are analog as well. The original incarnations of audio and video technology were also analog—and in some cases, still are.

Our world and bodies are analog, functioning in a continuous flow

Consider the process of recording and playing back sound on a cassette deck. Sound can be defined as fluctuations in air pressure that can be perceived by our ears with some qualitative attribute. That air movement is created by things like the human larynx, the vibrating membranes of

Cassette recording is an example of analog media

acoustic musical instruments, and the collision of objects. In cassette recording, those fluctuations of air pressure cause the microphone's metallic membrane to fluctuate analogously in an electromagnetic field, resulting in an analogous fluctuation in current through an electromagnetic head that causes an analogous rearrangement of the magnetic particles on the tape. The process is reversed on playback, replacing the microphone with a speaker that causes the air pressure to again fluctuate analogously. At the final stage, our eardrums vibrate analogously in a pattern that is recognized by the brain as being similar to the original sound.

Computers manipulate digital information as a discrete series of numbers

By contrast, the technology of the computer is fundamentally *digital*, defined as the representation of information as a series of numbers. Many recent developments in other media such as audio and video also employ digital technology. Audio CDs have virtually replaced vinyl records, for example. In the recording studios at the heart of the music industry, digital multitrack recorders and DAT (digital audio tape) recorders have made significant inroads into the domain of analog tape. High-end video production studios also employ digital technology in the form of digital switchers, effects devices, and recorders. In all of these cases, approximations of the analog information takes the form of a discrete series of numbers.

Digital media offer many benefits over analog counterparts

The benefits of digital over analog are significant, regardless of the medium. Numbers provide exacting control and repeatability. Where analog requires specialized circuitry for each type of signal manipulation, the altering of digital data merely requires the implementation of software routines. (As an example, a single digital signal processing chip can be preprogrammed to provide the functions of equalization, reverb, compression, and more that traditionally each requires dedicated analog devices.) Digital circuitry lends itself more readily to miniaturization. Storage devices and communication conduits capable of handling digital data can inherently accommodate any type of information taking digital form. Digital data lends itself to immediate random access. And digital information is not subject to degradation when stored, copied, or transmitted.

Getting Media In and Out of the Computer

Understanding digital technology is very straightforward when it comes to tasks such as spreadsheets, databases, and word processors to which numbers and alphanumeric characters are native. The inescapable fact, however, is that we humans can only directly create analog information, and only perceive digital information when it has been transformed into the analog domain. We are able to view spreadsheet numbers on a monitor only because the video display circuitry transforms the digital representation into analog signals that cause phosphor patterns to form in recognizable patterns on the screen. Conversely, computers can only generate and accept information in digital form.

Humans deal with analog information, computers with digital

The key to getting audio and visual information into the computer is the *analog-to-digital converter* (also known as an ADC or A-to-D converter). The A-to-D converter *samples* the analog signal level at regular intervals to construct a representation of the signal fluctuation over time—much like a movie camera takes a series of pictures to represent a moving image. Each sample is transformed into a number that represents that signal level. The *digitizing software* used to control the process collates the stream of numbers into an audio or video file type that can be stored, edited, manipulated, and integrated with other files when assembling the multimedia production.

Analog-to-digital converters allow real-world input

As you might expect, the *digital-to-analog converter* (also known as a D-to-A converter or DAC) provides the method of getting information back out. Here the stream of numbers from the audio or video files are transformed back into analog signal levels at the same rate at which they were originally sampled—much like a movie projector playing back the series of snapshots to provide the illusion of motion (see Figure 2.1).

Digital-to-analog converters output information our senses can assimilate

**FIGURE 2.1
Conversion between analog and digital formats**

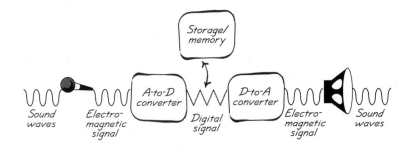

Two basic parameters are universally attributed to A-to-D and D-to-A
conversion and the associated files. *Resolution* (described in bits) determines the number of discrete digital levels used to represent the analog
signal—typically translating to dynamic range. For example, eight bits can
represent 256 values, hence 8-bit audio can represent 256 signal levels and
8-bit graphics can convey 256 colors. Sixteen bits can represent 65,536
values. *Sampling rate* (described in frequency) determines the number of
times the signal is sampled in a period of time—typically translating to
frequency response. Audio sampling rates of 44.1 kHz, for example, offer
twice the frequency response of 22 kHz sampling rates (see Figure 2.2).

**FIGURE 2.2
Relationship of
bit depth and
sampling rate**

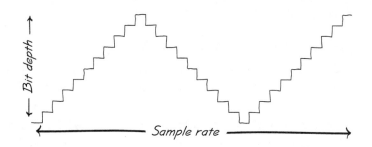

*Quality of
components directly
reflects the quality of
results*

People don't usually go out and buy pure ADCs and DACs, however—
they are part of the sound and video cards or circuitry used in multimedia
computing. Until recently the trend has been to add this input/output
capability to basic computers. The current trend is to add more and more
of these functions to the stock computer. What's important to know
about these components is that they and the related circuitry are not all
created equal. Like televisions, cars, or anything else, an inexpensive product that does the job doesn't necessarily offer the same quality results as a
version that incorporates better design, components, and potentially higher
price.

Factors Influencing Performance

*Playback must occur
in real time*

Information must flow through various pathways within the computer in
order to get from input stages to storage devices during media acquisition,
and from storage devices to output stages during delivery. While media
acquisition often takes place in steps, delivery typically relies on the real-
time transfer of data. As an example, one minute of high-fidelity video
may take several hours to digitize, but must still play back in one minute.

The capacity of data transfer during delivery is determined by many factors. *Access time* describes how fast the necessary information can be found on the storage media. *Transfer rate* refers to the speed at which data can be retrieved from the storage media to the main CPU. *Sustained transfer rate* describes the effective speed at which information can be continually accessed and transferred throughout the system—critical in a situation such as playing a long video file from a CD-ROM or hard disk. The speed of the other components such as the system bus, RAM, video display card, CPU, and operating system also influence performance (see Figure 2.3).

The speed at which data can be accessed and retrieved is a constraint

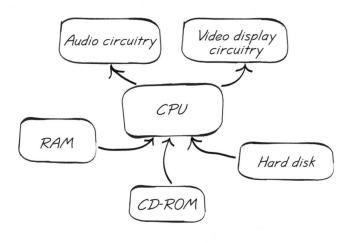

FIGURE 2.3 Basic flow of information through a computer on delivery

The interrelated concepts of bandwidth and throughput are more generic terms to describe the flow capacity of part or all of a system. *Bandwidth* basically refers to the capacity of the conduit. *Throughput* describes the maximum amount of information that can flow through that conduit in a given time—a major issue when dealing with the volume of data associated with multimedia. Moreover, the throughput of an entire system is determined by the throughput of the smallest or slowest conduit.

Combined pathways of data flow affect delivery speed

Analogies may help to visualize throughput limitations. If you visualize data in an electronic path as water in a pipe, all the water in the world will still only flow through a garden hose at the capacity of the hose. Conversely, visualize data as traffic on roads; traffic can easily slow and bottleneck when a highway goes from four lanes to two.

Water and traffic are examples of throughput

*Raw data/speed
ratios of multimedia
files often surpass that
of today's computers*

Put in context, the average microprocessor today can crunch through
from 25 to 60MB per second. The average system bus that accepts add-in
cards can handle only about 20 to 40MB per second. Typical hard drives
can transfer anywhere from about 350KB to 2MB per second, while a
double-speed CD-ROM drive sustains only about 300KB per second! As
you can imagine, this throughput disparity between interconnected and
interdependent conduits can cause bottlenecks in information flow. To
really put things in perspective, the entire text of this book usurps approximately 300KB of storage. Approximately the same amount of
information is required for a single color photograph large enough to fill a
monitor with moderate fidelity. Stereo CD-quality audio usurps 10MB
per minute. In contrast, raw digital video requires something on the order
of 27MB per second—a raging river compared to the garden hose of the
CD-ROM drive! (See Figure 2.4.)

**FIGURE 2.4
Throughput
ratios of
common
multimedia
elements**

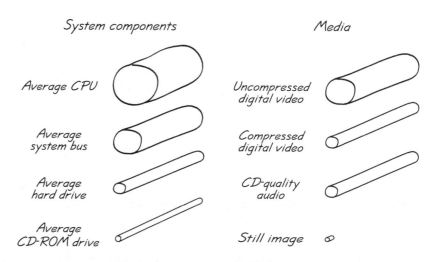

Special Processing with DSP

*Speed enhancements
have helped make
multimedia possible*

The major trend in addressing this issue is, of course, faster components
in every aspect of the computer—processors, hard drives, memory,
CD-ROM drives, system buses, and I/O buses. One of the more recent
solutions has been the inclusion of DSP (digital signal processor) chips,
which perform specialized functions at accelerated rates, such as audio and
graphics handling and speech recognition. While previously the domain
of add-on boards, some computers such as Apple's AV machines are
beginning to incorporate them directly on the motherboard.

Reducing Data with Compression

The large file sizes associated with multimedia would be prohibitive if not for *compression* technology. In fact, compression is one of the hottest growth areas within the multimedia manufacturing community. As you might guess, compression reduces the files to manageable sizes. There are various types of compression used according to the file type and presentation/delivery needs.

Compression technology reduces files to practical sizes

All types of compression have one thing in common—they must be decompressed in order to be viewed or played. Both the compression and decompression processes can take time and depend upon the nature of the file, compression technology, and processing power. Compression time isn't as great an issue since it takes place during production. Decompression, however, must appear seamless during the viewing process.

Files must be decompressed before playback

You unknowingly use basic compression technology each time you use a fax machine. A transmitting fax machine scans each line and sends a series of numbers telling the receiving machine the white, gray, or black value for each possible dot on the page. You've probably noticed that pages with little information on them fly through a lot faster than full ones. That's because fax machines use compression to send codes that effectively say things like "clear white line" or "80 white dots"—which is a lot faster to transmit than "white dot, white dot, white dot ..." and so forth. This same principle of using redundancy as a basis for compression is used in software like PK-Zip or StuffIt to fit a large file onto a floppy disk or reduce it for faster modem transfer. (Many modems now have this type of compression built in.) These redundancy encoding techniques are referred to as *lossless* compression because the information is represented exactly the same as the original when decompressed.

Lossless compression works by encoding redundancies

Lossless compression can often be used effectively to compress graphic files created within the computer, since lines and filled spaces often contain areas of solid colors or repeating patterns. Digitized photographs, on the other hand, don't compress well using the same methods. A blue sky, for example, may contain thousands of shades of blue. Since we actually only perceive a blue sky with some gradation, a different type of compression is used that averages areas of color and brightness according to how the human eye works. This type of compression that takes

Lossy compression works by averaging subtle differences

human perception into consideration is called *lossy* because information is actually discarded.

The advantage to lossy compression is that files containing complex information can be reduced to far smaller sizes than with lossless compression. The disadvantage is that information is indeed lost, causing potential degradation in the perceived results. The amount of compression determines the amount of reduction in both file size and quality (see Figure 2.5).

FIGURE 2.5 Compression ratios affect quality in lossy technology

Average quality   *Fair quality*

When Video Is Not Video

Computer-based video entails compromises

Lossy compression comes into play in multimedia primarily in the form of video compression. The underlying technology issues of digitizing and playing back video using computers is not trivial. The primary issue comes from the fact that video requires not only lossy spatial compression of photorealistic images, but temporal compression to handle the flow of as many as 30 of these images per second. To put things in perspective, the 27MB of raw video per second must be reduced to 300KB per second for delivery from common double-speed CD-ROMs. As described in Chapter 6, there are often compromises in image quality, image size, and the number of frames per second. In other words, video can indeed be integrated into multimedia computing, however the quality is not always up to the standards of traditional analog video.

Hardware decompression aids quality

Digital video technologies such as QuickTime and AVI are designed to handle these compromises. They provide for software-only playback of video from media such as hard disks or CD-ROMs. Quality can be significantly improved through the use of hardware decompression boards.

Chapter 6 also clarifies that the video signal itself is very different from computer display signals. By extension, computer signals can only be recorded onto videotape or displayed on a video monitor through the use of hardware that performs a conversion between these two signal types. Such products range in price from several hundred dollars to tens of thousands of dollars, with commensurate results. Although better-quality encoders can mask some design issues, it is advisable in general to avoid single-pixel horizontal lines and highly saturated colors. Conversely, images digitized from video signals will not be as pristine as a similar image digitized from a photograph using a scanner. The real point here is that computer and video display technologies are radically different, resulting in compromises when going from one medium to the other.

Additional hardware is required to convert output to traditional video

Multimedia and Networks

The bandwidth and throughput issues described earlier in this chapter impact the networking of multimedia. Different network types operate at different speeds. LocalTalk—the networking standard built into all Macintoshes—carries data at 230.4 kilobits/second. Ethernet—perhaps the most ubiquitous network protocol—operates at 10 megabits/second. In theory, a one-megabyte file that takes approximately 30 seconds to transfer via LocalTalk requires only about 1 second to send via Ethernet. These specs imply perfect conditions such as little to no simultaneous traffic on the network. Heavy network traffic and system messaging can significantly reduce these specs by as much as a factor of 10.

Most networks do not have the necessary bandwidth

Speed is less of an issue when files are being transferred for subsequent viewing. Real-time transfer is another matter, not just because of transfer rates, but because most entrenched networks are *asynchronous*—sending data without regard for time. These networks are designed to send the files you request as packets of data intermingled with packets of other people's files. The more files and messages being transferred simultaneously across the network and the larger they are, the more performance suffers. The bottom line is that, regardless of speed, the entrenched packet-switching network protocols were simply not designed to handle uninterrupted, synchronized real-time streams of data required for motion video and other dynamic multimedia elements.

Real-time transmission breaks packet-switching technologies

The solutions to networked multimedia in situations such as large corporations are threefold—in addition to compression. The first is to download content for subsequent viewing, thereby eliminating real-time issues. The second is to implement protocols that halt all other network traffic while a video is being viewed—a decidedly inelegant solution. The third and ultimate is for developers to create new *isochronous* (time-based) network protocols and layers that can support real-time video for purposes such as videoconferencing. They must also address the need to handle much heavier network traffic in the form of multiple real-time transfers of voluminous multimedia content throughout the corporate structure. FDDI II, SMDS, and BISDN are examples of emerging high-speed LAN and WAN protocols that facilitate isochronous transmissions. (These technologies are far from mainstream at this writing.) These protocols are largely reliant on fiber-optic cable since this medium offers as much as 25,000 times the bandwidth of copper wire (see Figure 2.6). Most of these emerging protocols are based on ATM, an international standard for data routing and transport.

FIGURE 2.6 Protocol solutions to streamed video on networks

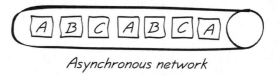

Asynchronous network

Video priority protocol

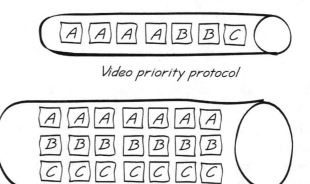

Full isochronous broadband network

Similarly, telecommunication of video and multimedia over traditional phone lines is limiting. The combination of several leased lines offering 64 kilobits/second on each channel have been an initial solution to basic videoconferencing and collaborative computing—although not fast enough to handle all multimedia applications. Most solutions to date have been available only by leasing dedicated lines in point-to-point configurations or by creating virtual corporate phone networks within the scope of the local phone network. The telephone companies' mandate is to expand services to significantly higher (better) bandwidths, make them as widely available as traditional phone service, and eliminate point-to-point restrictions. In doing so, they will share similar needs as computers for isochronous protocols and fiber optic cable. As seen in Chapter 16, the similar needs of many types of communication are fueling the development of the "information superhighway."

Telecommunications will require infrastructures similar to those in networks

3

Choosing Platforms and Media

On the surface, your choice of a computer platform for multimedia may seem as simple as the equipment already in your office. In an organization of any size, choosing a computer for multimedia just because it is the same as the ones currently used for business tasks is not necessarily prudent. Other factors may come into play. One obvious question is whether your existing equipment is up to the task. While spreadsheets, databases, and word processors can perform satisfactorily on machines of minimal power, both delivery and production of multimedia require much more computing horsepower. Further, equipment decisions must be separated into production and delivery machines.

Considerations in choosing computers for multimedia

The Cost of Production Machines

Purchasing considerations for computers used in multimedia production are different from those for delivery machines. Production systems invariably weigh in at a significantly higher price. For starters, storage requirements are significantly higher when creating media since there are often many source files and various stages of work in progress. (It is often advisable to acquire and manipulate source material at higher-quality levels than required for eventual playback, as this ensures that the materials can be edited or repurposed with the highest fidelity.) Many production systems incorporate one or more hard drives of 500MB to 1GB. Systems used for high-end video work often employ disk arrays—a series of parallel hard disks that function as a single, accelerated hard drive. More disk space and media also boost the requirements for back-up and archiving systems.

Production requires greater storage space

Similarly, additional memory translates to enhanced productivity. Multimedia source files can be quite large, and while many software tools used in multimedia production can utilize hard disk space as virtual memory, RAM is faster to access by orders of magnitude. Further, it is far more practical to have enough memory to keep several documents and

Additional memory can boost productivity

applications open during production rather than having to quit one to load another.

Production usually requires additional peripherals

While delivery machines have little need for media input, production machines usually require media acquisition hardware such as video digitizers, audio digitizers, MIDI interfaces, and flatbed scanners. The hardware to connect to these devices varies with ambition level, but includes possibilities such as video decks, camcorders, microphones, music synthesizers, and still-image cameras. Sophisticated multimedia production quickly incorporates many elements of traditional audio-video studios and art departments. CD-ROM drives are virtually indispensable for media library acquisition and production testing. Removable media such as Syquest, Bernoulli, and removable optical disks are quite useful in sharing media with team members. CD-ROM recorders are becoming increasingly popular as prices on these devices plummet and CD-ROM becomes more viable for mass delivery.

Speed equals productivity

For anything beyond simple presentations, the fastest machine available—from the processor on through the system buses, RAM, peripheral I/O, drives, DSP, and video display—will usually pay for itself in terms of time savings. Development machines must often crunch through significant amounts of information for tasks such as image editing, digital video acquisition and editing, audio processing, and 3-D rendering. In rendering a 60-second 3-D animation sequence, for example, the difference between the fastest and slowest processor on a Mac or PC might mean the difference between several days and more than a week!

Macs have led the field, but PCs are catching up

As for the choice of production platform, Macs have a strong track record—even in Windows title development. That's because multimedia tools were in place first on the Mac. Moreover, tools for graphic design, desktop publishing, digital audio, and MIDI sequencing matured on the Mac, causing it to be the popular production machine for these component media. (It's not unusual to see Macintoshes in the art department of an otherwise PC-based business.) As such, it has also endeared itself to more creative types contributing to multimedia than has the PC. On the other hand, the level of sophistication on the part of PC-based production tools has reached a formidable level.

Multimedia production can most assuredly be a cross-platform proposition. Ambitious productions often integrate the work of many people, and more file types than not can be translated either way between platforms. It is increasingly less crucial whether one artist uses a Mac and another uses a PC within the same project, for example.

Different platforms can be used for the same project

Things are a little less forgiving at the authoring level where the media components are integrated into the final production. There's no question that productions intended for Macintosh playback should be created on that platform. For PC delivery, it's usually better to go with the PC for production, unless Macs are already entrenched in your media production department. Productions designed for mass distribution on multiple platforms are typically created on the Mac, since more cross-platform authoring tools are in place. (There are fewer authoring packages that translate productions created on the PC to the Mac.)

Production platform choices vary with distribution goals

Multiple machines are typically used in sophisticated productions or large media departments—often mixing platforms. Beyond mixing Macs and PCs, Amiga and SGI machines can play important production roles. The Amiga becomes a powerful computer animation and analog video tool with the addition of Newtek's Video Toaster. The addition of Newtek's Screamer box can boost rendering of 3-D animation sequences by a factor of about 40. At this writing, Newtek's products are largely geared toward videotape output.

Amiga as a low-cost video production studio

SGI (Silicon Graphics) machines can offer similar performance boosts as dedicated computing environments. While the high-end SGI machines used for effects in the likes of *Terminator 2* and *Jurassic Park* can run $60,000 and beyond, entry models now start at under $5,000. Seemingly modest 3-D animation segments and large amounts of digital video can severely tax the average desktop machine, and many serious Mac and PC title developers use SGIs for rendering such segments. (To put things in perspective, George Lucas's ILM has a room containing dozens of networked high-end SGI machines that ran around the clock for months doing the dinosaur scenes for *Jurassic Park*.)

SGI machines offer serious power

The Cost of Delivery Machines

Multimedia requires more power than business applications

Delivery machines require a significantly lower investment than production machines. Nonetheless, that old 286 machine just won't cut it. In general, it seems that there is no such thing as too much speed, memory, or storage capacity. IBM's Ultimedia specification provides users of IBM-brand equipment with multimedia standards. In the PC-clone world, it is usually advisable to exceed the MPC (Multimedia Personal Computer) Level 2 specification as the minimum for delivery. In the Mac world, the low end of the Quadra line would be a recommended minimum. Regardless of platform, consider at least 8MB of RAM, a double-speed CD-ROM drive, and at least twice the hard drive capacity than you can imagine ever needing!

MPC Level 2 Minimum Specification

IBM PC or compatible with 25 mHz 486SX
4MB RAM
160MB hard disk
Graphic display with 65,000 colors at 640 × 480 pixels
CD-ROM drive (300KB/sec transfer rate, 400ms seek time)
16-bit, 44 kHz audio in/out with MIDI synthesizer
Joystick port
Microsoft Windows 3.0 with Multimedia Extensions 1.0

Public presentations may require additional power

If, for example, multimedia will play a major role in the everyday jobs of many employees—video mail, for example—you'll need to weigh the horsepower investment against productivity and aesthetics. When it comes to delivering state-of-the-art productions such as presentations or kiosks outside your organization, however, don't fool around. Outfit it to minimize bottlenecks at every turn. That includes the fastest processor, processor-direct or accelerated video card, preferably more than 8MB of RAM, at least a 240MB hard drive, and high-quality sound card and speakers. If anything approximating full-fidelity, full-frame, full-motion video is part of the equation, you'll also need a hardware video decompression card.

One other factor may influence your decision in terms of the computing power you invest in. That's the fact that pundits envision multimedia as something that everyone will do. It wasn't that long ago that word processing was a dedicated profession. The same is true to a lesser degree for desktop publishing. While it's doubtful that every employee will have the talent or mandate to pursue full-fledged multimedia production, audio-visual computing is likely to transcend telephony, fax, and other everyday communications. Technologies like voice recognition, desktop video conferencing, V-mail, and video publishing will require machine power similar to full-blown production machines.

Prepare for the future

It's no secret that PCs are the dominant computer in business. Given the power of today's hardware and software, there's no incredible reason to change platforms if your business is already based on PCs. PCs are also stronger than Macs in areas such as large networked databases. (Most multimedia support for PCs requires Windows or OS/2.) In the process of upgrading to PCs with faster processors, you'll have the option of buying multimedia-ready machines or adding multimedia upgrade kits. The latter may appear to be less expensive considering the bargain prices of the myriad PC clones. Consider, however, that the problems commonly associated with configuring the simplest of add-ons (things like hardware IRQ switch settings and memory management) will be multiplied when adding audio-visual capabilities to the typical PC. Given that time is money, purchasing turnkey systems may save money—and most assuredly headaches—in the long run. At the least, uniformity in upgrade kits is a recommended path in eliminating variables.

Turnkey multimedia PCs may be better than upgrades

If your business is not tied to PCs or is already Mac-based, consider Apple's offerings. Recent models have offered the same or greater bang for the buck as PC clones when taking multimedia into consideration. Apple debuted multimedia before Windows and continues its edge—Macs come equipped with built-in sound, color support, point-and-click interface, and software decompression. Apple's AV models go the extra mile with built-in inputs and outputs for sound and video in addition to DSP for more efficient processing of audio-visual data. The Mac is also still considered easier to learn, use, and modify than a PC at the level of the average user.

Macintosh offers a challenge to PCs

Alternatives in Delivery Media

Delivery method determines storage medium and playback

The sheer capacity requirements of multimedia lead to issues of storage and delivery media, which can be viewed in three basic scenarios. The first is that the production will be delivered from a computer over which you have complete control and which allows you to specifically tailor the production. This is often the case with business presentations or trade-show productions. The second is that you can specify a minimum configuration and ensure that the production runs under those constraints. This might be the case in distributing a sales presentation to field reps who all have at least that minimum configuration. The third is distributing a finished production to situations beyond your control, such as mass mailings of CD-ROMs to retailers or consumers. All too often the latter two situations lead to trade-offs between compatibility, capacity, production quality, cost, and speed.

Memory and Traditional Media

System memory offers the fastest throughput

The fastest and most costly storage area available to any computer is RAM (system memory). The average multimedia-capable computer has 8MB of RAM, several megabytes of which are typically usurped by the operating system, the multimedia application/player, and the file determining your production flow. Various multimedia delivery software packages use memory in different ways with regard to the actual media files. The greatest performance results from playing media files back from RAM by loading the entire production in memory before playback. Unfortunately, most productions incorporating any significant amount of media will quickly surpass the available RAM in the average desktop computer. While some systems will allow the addition of as much as 256MB of RAM, the cost of large amounts of memory can be prohibitive for everyday machines.

Large, fast hard drives and moderate RAM are optimal

Manufacturers have addressed this issue by developing audio and video file types designed to be played directly from storage media such as hard disks and CD-ROMs. Even so, graphics and animation must still typically be played from memory, often requiring the loading of files or segments as needed during playback. A fast hard drive with the necessary capacity and reasonable amounts of memory are thus the most practical way to go. Faster hard drives facilitate better video performance, better throughput of simultaneous media elements, and shorter load times for new media elements or segments. Greater RAM capacity permits creation and playback of more ambitious productions, requires fewer presentation delays associated with loads from disk, and allows multiple applications to be open during production. (Most computers dedicated to multimedia production and large-scale delivery have between 16MB and 128MB of RAM.)

Trade-offs become more of an issue when a production needs to be distributed. While floppy disks are both inexpensive and the lowest common denominator in an installed base, they are so slow that the production must usually be transferred to the user's hard drive for playback. Their small capacity also limits the size of the production, and installing files from more than one or two disks becomes tedious for the end-user.

Floppy disks: too small and too slow

Other removable media such as Syquest, Bernoulli, and removable optical technologies offer greater capacity in a portable package—anywhere from 44MB on up to 256MB (and even 1.2GB on the expensive side). Throughput in these media is often great enough for direct playback. The drawback is that they are costly and can only be accessed by someone with exactly the same drive technology. These media are often viable for intracompany situations such as distribution of tens of megabytes' worth of production to a dozen field offices who all use the same configurations.

Removable media lack widespread standardization

CD-ROM

With the exception of very expensive optical drive options, CD-ROM (Compact Disc–Read-Only Memory) currently offers the greatest capacity in removable media—as much as 650MB. Equally important, CD-ROM formats are reasonably standardized, the installed base is growing dramatically, and mass production is cost effective. In short, CD-ROM is the closest thing going to a standard in multimedia delivery.

CD-ROMs are best for mass delivery

Compact discs store the optical equivalent of digital data on microscopic tracks. As the disc spins at a fixed rate, a laser reads the optical information and associated technology, and the drive converts it to digital data. In addition to the incredible amount of information that can be stored optically in such a compact form (over 3000 copies of the text of this book, for example), the media is not susceptible to electromagnetic fields or any but the most severe physical damage.

Optical technology offers size, capacity, and durability

*CD-ROMs may
replace magnetic
media*

CD-ROMs are an extension of the audio CD that has replaced vinyl in
the music industry. Audio CDs hold digital data that only represent music.
CD-ROMs hold digital data that can represent any kind of data—audio,
graphics, animation, text, digital video, and computer programs. Any kind
of computer-readable content that can be put on a hard disk or floppy
disk can also be put on a CD-ROM. By extension, you need a compatible host machine because a PC file is still a PC file and a Mac file is still a
Mac file.

*The creation of CDs
entails a mastering
process*

Unfortunately, you don't just write to a CD-ROM like you do a magnetic
disk. The data must first be translated to the strict standards of the selected
CD format using specialized software. Then, specialized hardware is
required to make the actual CD or master. For mass production, a glass
master is first created that is then used to physically stamp out a large run
of plastic CDs. This process is facilitated at a handful of mastering plants
around the world using stringent tolerances, clean rooms, and megabuck
equipment. The process can be extremely cost effective in quantities—as
low as one dollar apiece in quantities of 1,000 or more. Shorter runs can
be accommodated using desktop CD-ROM recorders, currently available
in the $4,000 to $8,000 range. Since recordable CD media costs between
$14 and $30 per disc, this is practical only for short runs of several dozen
or less.

*CD-ROM's
weakness is speed*

The biggest drawback to CD-ROM technology is relatively slow transfer
rate. Performance varies depending on the speed of the drive. CD-ROM
drives adhere to the original spec transfer at 150KB/sec, while double-
speed drives provide 300KB/sec transfer rates. Manufacturers are racing to
ship drives with three, four, and five times the original transfer rate, significantly improving the viability of CD-ROM as a playback medium for
dynamic media. Developers incorporating video and/or animation usually
take one of two approaches: load files onto the delivery machine's hard
drive for playback, or optimize their content for a lowest common
denominator drive speed. In the case of software-only decompression, the
latter case has yielded video with major compromises in the areas of image
quality, image size, and frame rate.

CD-ROM Formats

- *CD-DA (Red Book)*—Standard digital audio CD. Doesn't require a computer, only an audio CD player. Holds up to 72 minutes of 16-bit digital audio at 44.1 kHz sample rate.
- *CD-ROM (Yellow Book)*—Superset of CD-DA. Capable of holding digital data representing any type of information. Data is proprietary to developer; formatting on CD is standardized. Red Book audio track(s) optional.
- *ISO 9660*—International standard extending CD-ROM directory access to multiple operating systems (platforms). Files still proprietary to developer and platform. Most often used to place Mac and PC versions of identical content on one CD-ROM.
- *CD-I (Green Book)*—Dedicated to CD-I stand-alone hardware player configuration designed for display on television sets. Proprietary operating system, video formats, and audio formats.
- *CD-ROM XA (Extended Architecture)*—Extension of CD-ROM dedicated to CD-ROM XA drive connected to a computer. Drive has audio decoder for standardized ADPCM audio providing range from 2 hours of LP vinyl quality to 19 hours of AM radio quality to 16 one-hour multilingual narration tracks. ISO 9669 access. Incorporates interleaving of audio and visual data for improved media synchronization.
- *CD-R (Orange Book)*—Recordable (writable) version of CD-DA, CD-ROM, and/or CD-ROM XA. Multisession (updatable) directory allows additional data to be added with subsequent writes.
- *Photo CD*—Kodak's proprietary version of ISO 9660 CD-R created from negatives and slides/transparencies at Kodak service bureaus. Originally designed primarily for display on TV via Photo CD, CD-I, Apple Power CD, 3DO, and other players; can also be accessed on Mac or Windows computers with appropriate software driver. Original *Master Photo CD* format accepts 35mm negatives and slides, and stores up to 100 photos in Image Pacs of 5 resolutions each. *Pro Photo CD* format accepts all film

continued

continued

types up to 4" × 5"; stores up to 25 photos in Image Pacs with 6*th* high resolution. *Portfolio Photo CD* allows authoring of interactive presentations using text, graphics, sound, and Photo CD images for service bureau mastering.

- *Video CD* (White Book)—Extension of CD-DA designed to play up to 74 minutes of MPEG-1 compressed video and audio. Designed primarily as linear delivery format for movies, but can be incorporated into interactive productions. Production requires costly compression technology; playback requires player or computer with inexpensive MPEG-1 decompression hard-

Other Delivery Options: Set-Top Players

Set-top players can also be used for multimedia delivery

One of the latest waves in consumer electronics is the proliferation of *set-top players*—stand-alone CD-ROM players designed to plug directly into TVs and video monitors. These are essentially computers disguised as home entertainment boxes. The keyboard has been replaced with a souped-up version of the familiar remote control, the media is read-only CDs, and the emphasis is on audience experience rather than do-it-yourself media creation. The long-range impact of this technology on the consumer market is discussed in Chapter 16. In the short term, these devices sometimes make sensible multimedia delivery platforms for business purposes.

Set-tops are inexpensive and simple to operate

The two major advantages are low price and simplicity. The consumer-market targeting of these units has yielded prices of between $500 and $1,000—lower than a PC clone outfitted for multimedia. Simple operation, combined with the ability to use any video monitor, makes them no-brainers for situations like a retail sales floor. In short, they offer more of the price and simplicity of a VCR than a computer.

Authoring and lack of computing power are problems

On the downside, content for set-top players must be authored indirectly on another computer system. Authoring tools for non-native delivery systems are few and far between, and testing and content modification ultimately mandates recording on CD-ROMs. Since part of the price/performance rationale of these systems is to bypass full-blown computing, there's little to no capability for input and storage of sophisticated user input, and off-the-shelf hardware options are scarce. Their best business use at this writing is therefore in mass-market automated marketing and merchandising presentations in situations such as chain store retailing, where cost effectiveness and stable messages are factors.

At this writing, there are only a handful of set-top players that are viable for delivery of business multimedia. The plethora of game machines from companies like Sega and Nintendo can largely be excluded because their development environments are proprietary and programming intensive. Other set-top players from companies like Atari are also coming on the market, but it's too early to tell their viability in delivering business media. Kodak's Photo CD players are perhaps the easiest for which to develop in that simple slide-show style presentations with music and/or narration can be authored on Macs with Kodak's inexpensive Portfolio software and turned into short-run CDs by service bureaus. As an added benefit, photographic slides and negatives can be used directly as source material. Photo CD is currently weak when it comes to dynamic elements such as animation, video, and synchronization, however.

Kodak's Photo CD is practical for slide/audio shows

Philips's CD-I offers more processing power for audio, graphics, animation, video, and interactivity than Photo CD. CD-I machines can also play Photo CD discs. MPEG 1 hardware decompression is also available in the form of add-on boards. CD-I discs are typically authored on Macs, usually with proprietary hardware that emulates the CD-I hardware. The stability of CD-I, combined with the ability to capture a small amount of user data, makes the platform a candidate for kiosks—although authoring complexities make it impractical for delivering most presentations.

Philips CD-I has more power

The other set-top player possibility at this writing is the 3DO format— the result of a collaboration between the likes of Electronic Arts, Matsushita (Panasonic), Time-Warner, and AT&T. The combination of processing power, special audio and graphics circuitry, and fast CD-ROM transfer rates make it a formidable delivery machine for entertainment titles. 3DO players can also access Photo CD discs. 3DO titles are currently developed in a Mac-based proprietary development environment

3DO is overkill for most businesses

running around $10,000. 3DO requires enough traditional programming to make it an unlikely platform for business delivery. As of this writing, Creative Labs is planning the release of a 3DO card for the PC and Macromedia has announced 3DO player software, paving the way for more mainstream uses of 3DO.

MPEG-based Video CD players will be used in the home

At this writing, inexpensive Video CD players based on MPEG 1 hardware decompression are making their debut. While these players are primarily aimed at replacing the VCR, some can also support a degree of interactivity. As such, they are most suited to situations requiring mainly linear video, possibly with some basic branching. The advantage over VCRs is that the hardware is much less subject to mechanical problems, and the media won't wear out. As with all MPEG technologies, creating CDs for these machines requires sophisticated compression technology that must be purchased or rented.

4

Graphics Tools

Technology Basics

The display of computer graphics (and video) relies on RGB (red, green, blue) technology, based on the principle that various combinations of red, green, and blue light can yield just about any color. The screens of computer monitors consist of a series of dots or pixels, each composed of a trio of phosphors that respectively glow red, green, and blue when energized. At the back of the picture tube are three electron guns that sweep across the screen in unison to energize each trio of phosphors in sequence. The signal levels of the three guns at any moment in time determine the intensity of the three phosphors of the current pixel, yielding a uniquely perceived color for that pixel.

Monitors use separate red, green, and blue signals

On the computer side, graphics files are copied from memory to the faster RAM in the display circuitry (see Figure 4.1) where an A-to-D converter transforms the digital data to three analog signals representing the brightness of the red, green, and blue levels. Those signals are sent through the cable to the monitor and routed discretely to the three electron guns.

The display adapter converts signals

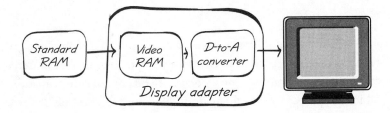

**FIGURE 4.1
Basic display
technology**

Color Resolution

Systems where the values held in memory directly correspond to the levels sent to the monitor use *direct color*. The current paradigm in high-quality graphics is 24-bit color resolution, where each of the three primary colors is represented by 8-bits of data per pixel. That yields 256 levels for each electron gun, combined for a total 16.7 million colors. The number of bits of resolution is often referred to as *color depth*. (See Figure 4.2.) This

Direct color offers the best color fidelity

type of direct color resolution is necessary for photorealistic graphics in print production, and desirable for the highest quality on-screen images as well.

FIGURE 4.2
Direct color
technology

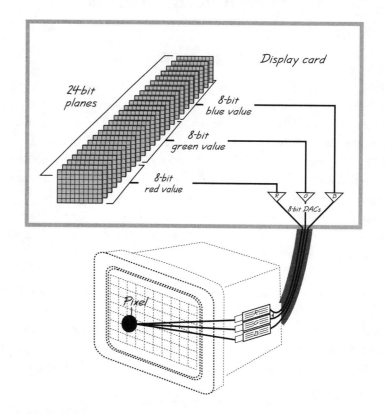

Alpha channels provide overlays

Graphics hardware and software often include extra data representing an *alpha channel* used to represent overlays for compositing images on screen. 32-bit graphics, for example, incorporates 24 bits of color information and 8 bits of alpha channel information, the latter representing 256 levels of transparency or 256 overlay colors.

Direct color is often too slow for multimedia

The problem is that 24-bit images take a while to shuffle through the system into the display circuitry and convert—too slow for most multimedia applications given current display technology. As a compromise, some display circuitry employs 16-bit color. This provides 1 bit of alpha channel information (on or off) and 5 bits (32 levels) for each color channel for a total of 32,768 colors. 16-bit color technology is found in many SVGA cards and in some Macintoshes. On most hardware, 16-bit color is still not fast enough for tasks such as smooth transitions and animation.

The standard compromise on most multimedia-ready machines is the use of 8-bit color. An 8-bit file requires one-third the storage and display time of a 24-bit file of the same physical resolution (before taking additional reduction via compression into consideration). Since 8 bits allows each pixel to have only one of 256 values, manufacturers employ the technique of *indexed color*. Here, each of the 256 values acts as an index to a position in a *color look-up table* that holds the actual value to be fed to the higher-resolution D-to-A converter. 8-bit indexed color allows for fast display of smaller files with 256 discrete colors that span the spectrum. Indexed color technology (see Figure 4.3) can also be implemented with lower bit resolutions, such as 4 bits for a 16-color palette.

Indexed color trades faster display for lower quality

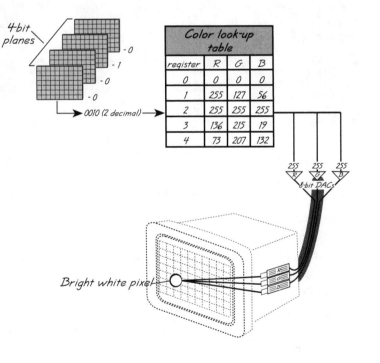

FIGURE 4.3
Indexed color technology

Spatial Resolution

The spatial resolution of a file or device is described in *dots per inch* (dpi). The average laser printer has an output resolution of 300 dpi, for example, while the average monitor displays either 72 or 75 pixels per inch in

Spatial resolution is measured in dots per inch

standard mode (see Figure 4.4). A standard monitor measuring 13" to 14" diagonally can display 640 pixels horizontally and 480 lines vertically—the size of the average full-screen multimedia image. (Multisync monitors can display higher resolutions.) Given a 1:1 ratio, an image that fills a 640 × 480 monitor screen would only take up about 2.13" × 1.6" on a laser printer page. Conversely, only a portion of a full-page printed image would fit on a monitor at 1:1 ratio.

FIGURE 4.4
Spatial resolution partially determines image quality

72 dpi   133 dpi

JPEG Compression

JPEG compression is a popular form of lossy compression

JPEG (pronounced "jay-peg" and short for Joint Photographic Experts Group) is the most entrenched form of lossy compression for photographic images. As with most lossy techniques, the user has some control over how much compression is applied. The greater the compression ratio, the more noticeable the artifacting will be. While purists often shun anything greater than a 2:1 through 5:1 ratio of original to compressed files, most people don't notice serious image degradation until ratios approximating 20:1—a significant reduction in file size.

Graphics Hardware

Display Hardware

Display hardware contains the circuitry used to hold the graphic image and convert it to analog signals to be sent to the monitor. The capabilities of the display hardware determine the color resolution such as 8-bit indexed or direct color at higher resolutions. (Most direct color hardware also includes indexed-color capabilities.) This hardware also dictates the monitor size that can be accommodated. In some products, these attributes can be boosted with the addition of extra VRAM (video RAM). Color depth and monitor size can sometimes be traded off within the same product. Display hardware might accommodate 32,768 colors at 640 × 480, for example; 256 colors at 800 × 600, and 16 color at 1,024 × 768.

Display hardware determines color depth and spatial resolution

Display hardware can be part of the computer's motherboard or take the form of a board residing in a card slot. All current Macintoshes, for example, have built-in motherboard graphics with at least 8-bit color depth. Display capabilities can often be enhanced with additional VRAM or a dedicated add-in card. PCs almost universally use the add-in card approach. Basic VGA (video graphics adapter) cards support up to 640 × 480 with 4-bit indexed color (16 colors). Most have *feature connectors* that accept add-on hardware to extend this to at least the 8-bit mode recommended for passable multimedia. SVGA (super video graphics adapter) cards offer a vast number of choices in terms of enhanced resolution and color depth.

Display hardware can be built in or added via a card

Speed is a major consideration in multimedia graphics display. Many cards now offer graphics coprocessors designed specifically to quickly crunch through image data. Even the fastest display circuitry is designed to fit in standard card slots and is still at the mercy of the typically slower system bus that transfers the image data from memory. Hence, the latest speed trend is the design of graphics cards that fit in the *local bus* of some PCs or the PDA (processor direct slot) of some Macintoshes. This technology allows the display adapter direct access to the microprocessor and memory.

The fastest adapters connect to the processor bus

Monitors

Monitors come in various physical sizes

All monitors are not created equal. Physical size (measured diagonally) is the most noticeable difference. (Some manufacturers measure the live image area, while others measure the entire visible area of the picture tube. Hence a monitor of a given size could be measured as 13" or 14", 16" or 17", 19" or 20", and so forth.) Unlike television and video monitors, larger computer monitors display more information rather than just making the same image larger. The standard multimedia presentation is designed for 640 × 480 pixels; the image area of a standard 13" or 14" monitor will do fine for basic multimedia delivery. Larger monitors can make life a lot easier during production, accommodating multiple programs and display windows. (Monitors or laptops with displays supporting fewer than 640 × 480 pixels are not recommended since most CD-ROM content is designed for this image area.)

Various scan rates and resolutions are supported

Regardless of physical size, various monitors are capable of different display resolutions as determined by their *scan rates*. Traditional monitors have fixed scan rates; *multisync* or *multiscan* monitors can accommodate a range of scan rates determining various resolutions, and are therefore more flexible. In either case the scan rate of the monitor must match that being output by the display circuitry.

Screen curvature and color control varies

The monitors offered by various manufacturers have different screen qualities. Most monitors exhibit a curvature that may seem to put your work in a bubble. Sony's Trinitron technology—licensed by a variety of manufacturers—uses a much flatter screen. Other manufacturers such as NEC are striving for flatter screens as well. More expensive monitors offer more sophisticated color correction controls that can be especially useful when the display is to be used for print production as well as multimedia.

Scanners

Flatbeds are the most popular scanners for flat art

Scanners are used to digitize existing photos and artwork into the computer. It is common for a business of moderate size to have at least one scanner already for OCR (optical character recognition) and scanning simple art like logos. Hand-guided models (approximately $400) can sometimes be used for occasional scans, but aren't well suited for production work. Flatbed scanners are the most common, and accommodate flat reflective art in much the same way as a photocopier. Most flatbeds today offer 24-bit color depth at 300 dpi minimum. Higher resolution is typically necessary only if the same scanner is to be used for sophisticated print production or you wish to acquire the highest-quality source material.

The popular range of flatbed scanners costs between $1,000 and $2,000; they are typically bundled with some form of image processing software. The quality of the results can vary widely between models. Higher *optical resolution* (actual hardware resolution) costs more money. A less effective but common practice is the use of hardware *interpolation* to boost the apparent resolution of the resulting file. The scanner comparison tests conducted regularly by computer magazines also evaluate for improper color casts, contrast, saturation, and detail in tonal ranges such as high-lights and shadows.

Hardware interpolation enhances resolution

Some flatbeds have an optional attachment for transparencies (around $500 to $800) which work to varying degrees of efficiency. Dedicated slide scanners starting at around $2,300 do a better job, but can't help with flat art. Art directors have routinely sent transparencies out to service bureaus for high-quality digitizing using a high-end *drum scanner*—typically $45 to $75 per scan. The resulting resolution is generally overkill for multimedia. Many people now send slides and negatives out to a service bureau offering Kodak's Photo CD service. This yields a CD-ROM with great quality images in several resolutions up to 3,072 × 2,048 for under $2 per image—including labor! For print production, the new Pro Photo CD format includes a 6,144 × 4,096 high-res version for about $15 per image.

Kodak Photo CD is an alternative to scanning film

Still-Image Digital Cameras

Digital cameras employ the same basic technology as camcorders to acquire images, but instead record still images to memory or disk. From there the images can be transferred to the computer for use with the standard array of programs (sometimes requiring a proprietary input card). The major advantage is instant access to pictures without waiting for developing and scanning. Unfortunately, the resolution is only that of video, so it's not much help in other applications such as print production. Control and contrast are equivalent to modest camcorders at best. These

Average digital cameras offer only video resolution

still-image cameras like the Canon Zapshot range from about $700 to $1,200 and are best suited for situations such as real-estate or security databases where high volume and fast acquisition are more important than image quality.

High-end digital cameras are justified for special applications

The contrast, resolution, and optical control that photographers are accustomed to is available in digital SLRs (single-lens reflex) in the $4,000 to $13,000 range. While professional digital photography at affordable prices is coming, it is typically justified today only by some photojournalists and photography studios. Currently, the best photographic price/performance results are still yielded from digitizing high-quality photographs. The more expensive, high-resolution versions are designed primarily for studio use.

Graphics Tablets

Graphics tablets lend an artistic feel to graphics

Graphics tablets provide an alternate input to the mouse when creating and editing graphics. The tablet's surface is responsive to the positioning of a pen-like stylus, allowing the user much more intuitive control in creating expressive strokes with paint and image processing software. Most current models also transmit information corresponding to the pressure applied. This data can be mapped to various painting parameters such as brush size, opacity, and color for highly desirable levels of expression. Decent graphics tablets start at street prices under $400.

DSP Cards

DSP cards can accelerate some tasks

DSP cards have special DSP (digital signal processor) chips on them that can accelerate certain processing-intensive tasks. Custom software drivers must be written by application manufacturers in order to divert these tasks to the DSP and perform them. The most popular to date is the acceleration of selected Adobe Photoshop tasks and filters; however, manufacturers of digital video, audio, and telephony software are beginning to take advantage of this technology as well.

Graphics Software

Image Processors

Image processing software, such as Adobe Photoshop and Aldus PhotoStyler, is often bundled with scanners to facilitate cleaning up and altering scanned images. (They can be purchased separately as well for about $500.) Image processors are the digital equivalent of the photographer's darkroom. Selection tools are incorporated that are designed for isolating specific portions of photorealistic images for further manipulation. Basic operations akin to those of the darkroom include adjusting brightness, contrast, density, color balance, saturation, positive/negative, size, cropping, orientation, and rotation. They also excel at selective compositing of multiple images including the use of transparency and masks.

Image processors primarily manipulate scanned images

For multimedia, these tools also provide for altering resolution for screen display, converting from high-resolution direct color to 8-bit indexed color, and converting between myriad file types. While image processors are largely designed to perform operations on existing areas, many offer enough artistic tools to be used for image creation as well. A growing trend is the proliferation of digital filters that perform transformations such as embossing, solarizing, edge tracing, spherizing, twirling, texturizing, and painterly stylization (see Figure 4.5). Many of these take the form of third-party software accessories (typically around $100 per set) compatible with the image processor's *plug-in* (expansion) technology. Plug-in technology can also be used to add hardware support for various input and output devices.

DSP can also perform a variety of special effects

**FIGURE 4.5
Examples of
image
processing
effects**

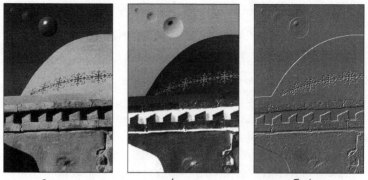

Original   Invert   Emboss

Find edges   Charcoal   Pond ripples

Paint Software

Paint software is used to create bitmap graphics

Paint software such as Mathematica's Tempra Pro is designed to provide the tools for computer graphics staples such as lines, circles, rectangles, polygons, and freehand strokes—complete with color fill, gradient fill, and pattern fill options. Some packages only work with indexed color, while more advanced versions support higher-resolution direct color. Some products also support some of the basic darkroom control and plug-in technology afforded by image processors. (Image processors are still highly recommended for tasks such as altering resolution.) Ballpark price range is $100 to $300.

Packages that emulate natural artistic media are popular with artists

The past few years has seen heated momentum in paint packages such as Fractal Design's Painter that emulate true canvas, paint, and artistic expression—especially when used in conjunction with a graphics tablet and a trained eye and hand. Media such as oil, watercolor, chalk, pencil, felt tip, and ink can be selected, and brush size, shape, consistency, and response adjusted to incredible degrees of control. Preset styles can even help the user emulate the techniques of masters like Van Gogh and Seurat (see Figure 4.6). Surface textures ranging from paper to concrete can be applied, as well as basic lighting. While these tools don't do all the work, they open incredible potential for creative expression. Prices are about $300, and the investment in a graphics tablet is wise.

FIGURE 4.6
Example of a painterly style using Painter and a graphics tablet

Drawing and Illustration Software

Image processors and paint programs manipulate the individual pixels that comprise the image. In general, the resulting *bitmap* is cast in stone until erased or painted over because it is based on individual pixels rather than mathematical shapes. *Drawing software* and *illustration programs* differ from paint programs in that each element created retains its own identity—a technology known as *object-oriented* or *vector* graphics. That means that objects can be selected, moved, scaled, rotated, deleted, and otherwise manipulated without affecting the rest of the image (see Figure 4.7). This flexibility is very much welcome while establishing a design or in tasks such as creating charts that are subject to change. The trade-off is that the results are typically not very photorealistic or painterly, exhibiting more of sharp "computer graphic" style.

Objects created with vector graphics retain their identity

FIGURE 4.7
Objects preserve their identity with vector graphics

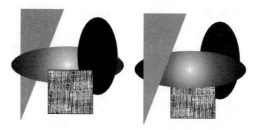

Drawing programs primarily create graphics for desktop output

There is a subtle difference between draw and illustration programs. Draw programs such as CorelDraw are typically designed for generic use with on-screen graphics and desktop printers. They often ship with large libraries of clip art, reflecting more orientation toward the novice. Drawing programs start at next to nothing and range up to $500—depending on features and included libraries.

Illustration programs excel at driving high-resolution output via PostScript

Illustration programs like Adobe Illustrator and Aldus Freehand are typically used to create original art in PostScript format. While PostScript (a page description language) is implemented on many desktop printers, it is the format of choice for outputting files on high-end imagesetters in print production work. While few media integration packages use PostScript files, it's easy enough to convert PostScript files to bitmap files. If the same equipment is to be used for print production and object-oriented multimedia graphics, an illustration package would probably be a better choice over a drawing program. (There's plenty of PostScript clip art from the desktop publishing world.) Illustration programs sell for around $400 to $500.

Animation Software

Animated cartoons employ cel animation

2-D animation software takes several forms, but universally refers to products that apply motion to flat two-dimensional drawings. Classic animation techniques seen on TV cartoons utilize *cel animation*. Disney's Animation Studio (around $100) is one of the few packages that caters to this specialized genre where characters and their body parts move expressively over scrolling backgrounds. This package facilitates the classic "onion skin" technique used to visualize previous frames while drawing.

Object animation programs, such as Autodesk Animator and Cinemation, are the mainstay of computerized 2-D animation. They move multiple graphic objects around the screen over a background (see Figure 4.8). Simple objects can be drawn within the program or more complex ones imported from other graphics software—typically at 8-bit resolution. Control is typically provided for overlay priority, rotation, flips, blending, and the like. Motion paths allow the user to specify the start and end point across a range of frames and have the computer fill in the gaps. Street prices range from $300 to $500. This type of animation is increasingly being integrated into presentation and production packages, discussed later in Chapter 7.

Most computer-based animation moves objects over a background

FIGURE 4.8
Object animation

3-D Software

While 2-D software manipulates flat images, *3-D software* manipulates representations of three-dimensional objects in a representation of three-dimensional space. 3-D modeling software is used to create geometric wire-frame objects that have length, breadth, and depth. These can also be joined to create more complex objects. Some packages like Macromedia's MacroModel are designed to create more organic shapes through the use of curves and "Silly Putty-like" point stretching.

3-D graphics are representations of objects and space

Objects are then positioned in the scene and given surface attributes such as color and texture (such as wood or metal) with various degrees of reflective and translucent qualities. 2-D graphics or photos can also be mapped onto surfaces and backgrounds. Light sources are positioned in relation to the objects and given attributes such as brightness, color, and diffusion. Finally, a virtual camera is positioned that represents the user's viewpoint. When all this is set up, the scene is *rendered*—a process that creates a realistic image based on all the parameters (see Figure 4.9). Rendering a single frame can take anywhere from an hour to several days depending on the complexity of the scene, output size, resolution, and computing horsepower.

A scene is created by choosing objects, surfaces, lights, and viewpoint

**FIGURE 4.9
Rendering of a
wire-frame
model**

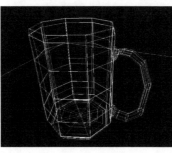

Wire-frame model   *Rendered image*

*Some packages
integrate all the stages
of 3-D work*

Some manufacturers offer packages dedicated to the individual steps of modeling, staging, and rendering. Pixar's Showplace, for example, specializes in scene creation, while variations on their Renderman product only provide the final rendering process. Others integrate all three phases. Due to the processing requirements for rendering, more manufacturers are offering *distributed rendering* engines that can use any available computer on a network to perform parts of the rendering task. Basic 3-D software starts at as little as $300, but rapidly climbs into the thousands.

*Not all 3-D packages
support animation*

3-D animation extends this genre of tools for the kinds of moving parts and fly-through effects seen in the opening logos of network TV movies, commercials like those from Intel and Listerine, and architectural walk-through. The objects, lights, and cameras can all typically be given motion paths—making it possible to simulate just about anything one can imagine (see Figure 4.10). Some even support the ability to metamorphize one object into another, as popularized in *Terminator 2*. While a few companies offer less expensive products, complete 3-D animation systems for common desktop computers typically go for a minimum of around $1,000 and can climb as high as $7,000 for advanced capabilities.

FIGURE 4.10
3-D animation

*Serious 3-D
animation requires
serious computing
power*

The negative side of 3-D is that rendering even modest sequences can tie up computers for days and even weeks. That—along with the decidedly different discipline required for creating scenes via modeling—explains why you don't see much 3-D animation in everyday business productions. 3-D animation is the single most compelling reason to invest in one or more high-end machines for rendering. Unfortunately, the software investment is often as much as that required for the hardware, with packages for UNIX machines like SGI starting at around $7,000 and climbing into the tens of thousands! An investment in this level must obviously pay for itself in terms of ongoing 3-D needs. If a single production calls for more 3-D work than your equipment can handle, consider contracting out those segments to a service bureau or video production firm who has already made the investment.

Graphics Conversion Software

*File conversion should
be part of every
producer's tool kit*

At the simplest level, graphics conversion software can transform a graphics file from one format and/or platform to the desired one. This is especially helpful in cross-platform work. Some image processors like Adobe Photoshop input and output a reasonable number of graphic formats, as can some generic file-conversion utilities such as HiJaak. A more sophisticated application like Equilibrium's DeBabelizer goes the extra mile with features like palette translation/reduction and batch processing of many image editing features—very handy when converting a number of source images into a format for multimedia integration.

Clip Art and Stock Photography

Clip art libraries are indispensable for nonartists

Often the cost and skills associated with creating the requisite elements of a production are prohibitive. Designers and video producers relied on canned media for decades before the multimedia revolution. During the desktop publishing boom, books of printed clip art gave way to similar libraries in PostScript form. Countless companies advertise these disks and CD-ROMs in the back of computer and graphic design magazines such as *Publish*. Moreover, many manufacturers of graphics and multimedia software are waging a war over who can bundle the most clip art free with their products.

Stock photo agencies provide images of just about anything

Stock photography has a similar story. Originally, an art director would either flip through massive stock photo catalogs or call a stock agency researcher directly to find the right image, buy the rights to use the image in a specified circumstance, and then pay to have the film rush delivered. Multimedia rights for a one-time trade-show production average around $200 to $300 per image. Now some traditional stock houses sell a catalog of screen-resolution images on inexpensive CDs as comps (most suitable for multimedia), then perpetuate their time-honored traditions for high-res film for print production. Newer stock houses that are more multimedia savvy often place hundreds of screen-resolution (and even high-res versions) on CDs. For around $300 per disc, you can use the images in just about any way you choose. These comparatively inexpensive libraries can be invaluable in creating marketing productions. Some companies are also beginning to create stock services on-line.

Fonts

Fonts communicate subconscious statements

While fonts may seem pedestrian in contrast to glitzy multimedia tools, the power of typography should not be underestimated. Designers and art directors know that fonts make subliminal statements ranging from casual to formal, masculine to feminine, fun to elegant, and much more (see Figure 4.11).

The Store   **The Store**

**FIGURE 4.11
Fonts make
subliminal
statements**

THE STORE   the store

The Store   THE STORE

Some companies offer libraries of dozens and even hundreds of fonts for as little as a few dollars per font. Companies such as Adobe, Letraset, and AGFA, who distribute typefaces created by high-end designers, often charge more like $50 for a few selected fonts. Given the expanse of these libraries, entire collections can be worth over $10,000. To compromise the issues of price and access, these firms have taken to placing encrypted versions of their entire libraries on CD-ROM. When you want to buy a specific font, you call an 800 number with your credit card and the company gives the code to unlock the desired font.

A library of fonts are sometimes encrypted on CD-ROM

Fonts come in two basic flavors today—PostScript and TrueType. PostScript fonts came first and are the staple of most designers and service bureaus dealing with print production. If you need fonts to do double duty, buy PostScript. TrueType is a standard introduced by Apple and adopted by Microsoft that works fine for most applications and is often inexpensive. Programs such as Altsys's Metamorphosis can convert between the two formats if necessary.

Users must choose between PostScript and TrueType

Recently, the manipulation of type has become a popular design trend. Image processing, drawing, and illustration software can perform operations such as stretching and rotating. Some drawing software such as CorelDraw can place type in an envelope that allows the shape of entire words to be manipulated. Illustration programs like Adobe Illustrator can fit type into a curve or path. Brøderbund's Typestyler specializes in

Font manipulation adds interest to typefaces

creating these effects as a stand-alone package. Pixar's Typestry is an example of programs specializing in creating 3-D type effects, including path animation. (See Figure 4.12.)

FIGURE 4.12
Type manipulation tools can yield interesting titles

5

Audio Tools

Digital Audio Basics

All digital audio is not created equal. The quality of digital audio is measured according to two basic parameters—resolution and sampling rate. Resolution determines the number of bits used to represent the dynamic range—the difference between the softest and loudest sounds. (One of the things that distinguishes a cassette recording from an audio CD, for instance, is that the latter has about twice the dynamic range, which makes the content sound, well—more dynamic!) 8-bit audio has the approximate dynamic range of a cassette, 12-bit produces that of an LP, and 16-bit offers the dynamic range found in CDs (and approximating that of the human ear).

Audio resolution dictates dynamic range

Sampling rate determines how many pieces of data each second are used to represent the sound, measured in kilohertz (kHz)—or thousands of cycles per second. Without getting overly technical, the frequency response of the audio will be half that of the sampling rate. People with perfect hearing can hear frequencies (pitches and overtones) up to about 20 kHz. CD-quality audio has a sampling rate of 44.1 kHz, resulting in content that contains all of the audible frequencies. Another common sampling rate is 22 kHz, yielding frequency response of about 11 kHz—a little better than AM radios and telephones. While higher sampling rates are desirable for music, this lower rate is acceptable for conveying the frequencies found in human speech.

Sampling rate dictates frequency response

Resolution and sampling rate determine the size of a digital audio file, potentially usurping a reasonable amount of storage space and bandwidth. On the low end, 8-bit, 22 kHz in mono translates to 1.25MB per minute. On the high end, 16-bit, 44.1 kHz in stereo requires 10MB per minute.

Higher resolution and sampling rates yield larger files

MIDI Basics

MIDI is a protocol for controlling electronic musical instruments

MIDI (pronounced "mid-ee" and short for Musical Instrument Digital Interface) provides a very low-bandwidth alternative to digital audio for music and sound effects. MIDI is a communication protocol for controlling music synthesizers—whether they are stand-alone, built into a PC sound card, or embedded in software as with QuickTime 2.0. You can think of the synthesizer as an orchestra and the controlling MIDI data as the conductor with the musical score. (The MIDI file might also be likened to a player piano roll.) MIDI data essentially tells the synthesizer which notes to play, when, how long, what sound to use, and with what expression. This performance data requires something on the order of only 50KB per minute—a significant reduction in storage and throughput requirements.

General MIDI standardizes a palette of sounds

Until recently, electronic music manufacturers had standardized MIDI control but not sounds. The recent General MIDI addendum to the MIDI spec maps out a specific palette of sounds that allows developers to arrange compositions for the equivalent of an orchestra with known seating. You can always get a piano sound by calling program 1, for example, and a violin by calling program 41. Not all synthesizers comply with the General MIDI spec.

Audio Hardware

The recording and broadcast industries have spawned a vast array of audio hardware. We'll review the primary subset used in everday multimedia.

Sound Cards

PCs require sound cards for audio input and output

While Macs have always had some form of built-in digital audio output circuitry, and later models also sport internal audio input, most PCs require the addition of a sound card in order to support audio. Most offer both input and output capability. While there is a large installed base of 8-bit, 22 kHz boards, most of today's new sound cards offer 16-bit, 44.1 kHz on both recording and playback for as little as $150. These specs are highly desirable for multimedia production work.

Part of what differentiates sound cards is the nature of the inputs and outputs. Many lack line-level input and output jacks. Cards with only microphone-level inputs won't do as good a job digitizing line-level signals; conversely, those with only headphone outputs aren't optimized to drive sound systems. Regardless of the physical connections, anything less than top quality in the input preamp and output amplifier circuitry can affect the signal-to-noise ratio, bringing the audio quality to significantly less than that of a CD.

Input and output circuitry affects sound quality

The synthesis capabilities of sound cards vary depending upon the OEM chipset used. In all, the number of voices (notes) that can sound simultaneously essentially determines how large your orchestra is. Yamaha originally introduced FM (frequency modulation) synthesis technology to the market. The number of operators in FM synthesis determines the potential sonic complexity and realism. The popular original Creative Labs' Sound Blaster employed Yamaha two-operator chips with 11 voices. The current Yamaha chip offers four operators with 20 voices. Several other OEM chipsets employ 24- to 32-voice *wavetable* synthesis, which uses digital samples of actual instruments for greater realism. Most cards offer standard or optional MIDI connectors to connect keyboards and other musical devices.

Several types of synthesis can be found on sound cards

Most PC sound cards also include direct audio connections for CD-ROM drives. Some also incorporate the necessary controller for the CD-ROM drive. Sound cards also incorporate mixers that can combine the available sound sources. This often includes live microphone input—handy for live presentations. Sound cards are now often purchased as part of an MPC upgrade kit.

MPC-compatible sound cards are now available

Audio Digitizers

All models of Macintosh and Amiga have either 8-bit or 16-bit internal audio and audio output capabilities. Later models of Macintosh also have audio input built into the motherboard. Earlier models can acquire sound via dedicated *audio digitizers* such as Macromedia's MacRecorder, which has a rudimentary internal microphone as well as line-level input.

Early Macs may require an audio digitizer

Direct-to-Disk Recorders

*Direct-to-disk
recorders provide
professional sound*

Direct-to-disk recorders typically up the ante over internal audio circuitry and garden-variety sound cards. These products have professional studio-quality specs, handle more of the processing onboard, and often include built-in DSP for faster editing operations. Products like Digidesign's Audiomedia II and Turtle Beach's 56K also offer professional digital input and output for direct connection to DAT recorders and other pro-level digital audio products. Synchronization to audio and video decks is included on better products. Prices range between $1,000 and $3,000.

*Better systems
provide more than
two tracks of digital
audio*

More expensive versions such as Digidesign's Pro Tools II raise the bar from two-track mastering quality to digital multitrack recording with four or more tracks. While these are designed more for recording studios, they can be of great value when recording, editing, and mixing complex soundtracks. Prices start at around $5,000.

Stand-Alone Synthesizers

*Synthesizers can be
added with a MIDI
interface*

Since Mac setups don't usually require additional cards for digital audio, they don't automatically get the benefit of on-board synthesis. A wealth of MIDI synthesizers (with and without keyboards) and related products are available from the music industry that created and lives by MIDI. These can also extend the MIDI orchestration capabilities of PC sound cards. Several inexpensive models like Roland's Sound Canvas are oriented toward computer users and start at under $500. An inexpensive MIDI interface for the computer (under $100) or built into a sound card is required in order to communicate with external MIDI devices.

Powered Speakers

*Most multimedia
speakers include small
power amps*

Most sound cards and audio output circuits found in computers put out a preamplified signal level capable of driving headphones or an amplifier to drive speakers. Most speakers for multimedia therefore incorporate small amplifiers. Selection of powered speakers should be determined by the overall power and frequency response required for a given system, as well as a listening test. Many manufacturers provide the ability to mix between multiple audio inputs for situations requiring several audio sources such as microphones, VCRs, CD, and computer-based audio. Note that major presentations require greater power amplification and larger speakers, usually in conjunction with mixer-based P. A. systems.

Microphones

Different microphones are designed for specific tasks. The microphones included with some computers, sound cards, and tape decks are typically too cheap to do any serious production work. Most situations require a *unidirectional* microphone because this design accepts sound from the front and rejects most of it from the sides and rear. (The only time an *omidirectional* design is appropriate is in recording ambient sound from all directions or covering a crowd.) (See Figure 5.1.) Presenters and video spokespeople benefit from unobtrusive clip-on *lavalier* microphones, available in both wired and wireless designs. Noisy environments such as trade shows sometimes require the use of headset microphones in order to eliminate background din. Decent mics for these purposes run between $100 and $400. Other specialized mics are recommended for recording specific instruments, vocals, and stereo sound effects.

Choose the right microphone for each situation

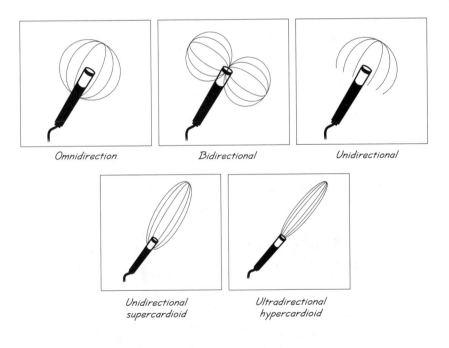

Omnidirection   Bidirectional   Unidirectional

Unidirectional
supercardioid

Ultradirectional
hypercardioid

**FIGURE 5.1
Polar patterns
determine what
microphones
pick up**

Other Audio Tools

The world of audio equipment is vast and potentially complex. Categories include DAT recorders for acquisition and mastering, analog and digital multitrack tape decks for layering many tracks in composition and soundtrack production, mixing consoles for selective combining of tracks and

An array of professional studio equipment can be used

sound sources, signal processors for tone control and special effects, and much more. Most of these tools are beyond the needs of everyday multimedia and fall in the domain of the recording studio. Perspectives on these tools and their use can be found in *The Desktop Multimedia Bible*.

Audio Software

Sound editing software largely falls into the categories of digital audio and MIDI.

Sound Editing Software

Waveform editors are staples

Sound editing software allows viewing and manipulation of digital audio waveforms (see Figure 5.2). Basic cut and paste operations on products like Voyetra's AudioView and Opcode's AudioShop can be used for trimming out unwanted silence or words, as well as shortening or lengthening music to fit a visual passage. Various products offer signal processing, including simple fade-ins and fade-outs, echo, reverb, and level normalization. Basic sound editors start at under $100, although care should be taken to get a package that supports the file format, resolution, and sampling rate of your audio hardware.

FIGURE 5.2
Waveform editing with Sound Designer II

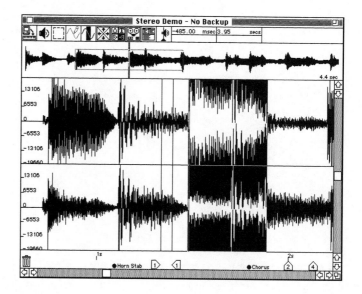

Advanced products like Digidesign's Sound Designer II ($995) feature nondestructive editing and playlists that retain the original sound file and merely perform random-access playback for a variety of mix arrangements. Other advanced features include studio features like equalization, compression/limiting, pitch shifting, time compression/expansion without altering pitch, seamless looping, stereo panning, location markers and more. These tools may be overkill for everyday multimedia, but invaluable for serious audio work.

Advanced editors offer more control

MIDI Sequencers

MIDI sequencers are used to create and edit the MIDI sequence files that tell synthesizers what to play. They employ a model similar to a multitrack recorder where each parallel track typically contains the performance of a given instrument (see Figure 5.3). Most business producers will use sequencers themselves only to alter prescored sequences, changing the length, arrangement, tempo, or instrumentation.

Sequencers create and edit MIDI files

MIDI sequencers like Opcode's Vision and Passport's Master Tracks are powerful composition tools that control anything from a single synthesizer to an entire recording studio. In fact, many major recording artists use MIDI sequencers more than tape these days. Musical ability and a moderate studio set up is typically required in order to do much with these tools. If you just need original music for an occasional project, there are plenty of producers and composers who have the talent and equipment to deliver one without requiring an investment in additional audio equipment.

Sequencers are primarily used by composers

FIGURE 5.3
MIDI sequencers serve as virtual multitrack recorders

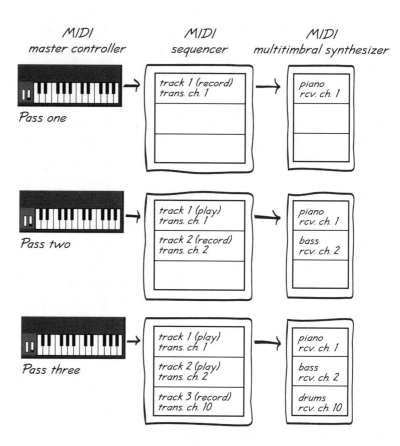

Music and Effects Libraries

Library music can save time and money

As with clip art and stock photos, music libraries have long serviced the needs of media producers. Most music libraries sell audio CDs with many tracks in a "buy-out" arrangement (under $100 each) where you are free to use it in nonbroadcast productions. (Broadcast rights can be negotiated.) Better libraries offer variations on each theme that can be used for long and shorter passages, as well as transitions. There are just as many companies offering CDs full of sound effects. The advent of multimedia has also caused some libraries to offer CD-ROMs with material in file formats that can be brought directly into the computer. There are also some clip MIDI sequences of original music designed specifically for multimedia, and a good number of sequences of cover songs are advertised in musicians' magazines like *Keyboard* and *Electronic Musician*.

6

Video Tools

Basic Video Concepts

While the computer world refers to video in association with display adapters and monitor signals, the signals driving computer monitors are significantly different from the video standards used in television, VCRs, and broadcast. Similarly, "video" files on the computer screen may provide the basic appearance of video, but are not technically video in the broadcast and consumer electronics sense. The differences in the two types of signals underpin many of the technologies associated with digital video.

Computer video differs from traditional video

Several parameters are implicit in the video standard, which makes it possible to freely interconnect various video devices such as camcorders, VCRs, and monitor. First, true video operates at a fixed frame rate. Second, video is overscanned, meaning that the image extends under the cosmetic front mask to the edge of the picture tube. (This calls for a *safe titling area* whereby titles are restricted to the inner 80 percent of the screen.) By contrast, computer images always have an inherent border. Third, a video frame is actually made up of two *interlaced* fields consisting of the even and odd scan lines, respectively. Computers display a series of single noninterlaced fields each consisting of all sequentially drawn lines (see Figure 6.1).

True video relies on rigid standards

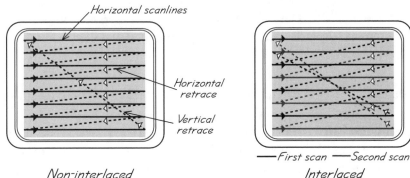

Non-interlaced

Interlaced

FIGURE 6.1 Differences between video and computer display technology

Different parts of the world use different standards

There are also several video standards in use around the world. The NTSC (National Television Systems Committee) standard is used in North America, Central America, Japan, and parts of South America and the South Pacific. The PAL (Phase Alternation Line) standard is entrenched in the United Kingdom, West Germany, The Netherlands and some other parts of the world. SECAM (Sequential Couleur Avec Memoire) is employed in France, the former Eastern bloc, and parts of the Middle East. HDTV (High Definition Television) is still undergoing a standardization process.

Broadcast video suffers additional image degradation

All of these standards were initially developed for television broadcasts. While color video cameras and monitors operate internally on a combination of signals representing the red, green, and blue values of colors, the aforementioned video standards require an additional encoding and modulation process in order to be broadcast. This adds a level of degradation with respect to both resolution and color fidelity. You may have noticed, for example, that some colors such as bright red will appear to bleed on even the best TVs. Some modern equipment alleviates some (but not all) of this artifacting by allowing direct connection of video gear via *component video* connections rather than *composite video* connections (the former also known as *S-video* on consumer-level gear). Component video carries the native video signal without the extra degradation associated with the modulation required for broadcast.

Video Compression

Computerized video must be compressed

Given that NTSC video in North America and some other parts of the world runs at 29.97 fps (frames per second), one second of raw video totals about 27MB. This volume requires serious compression in order to accommodate even the fastest of desktop computers and hard drives, let alone CD-ROM transfer rates.

Image size, fidelity, and frame rate are trade-offs

While still images only require *spatial compression*, the throughput requirements of video bring the added need for *temporal compression*. The added dimension of time is typically addressed by storing a *key frame* containing a full image at periodic intervals, then keeping track of only the differences between the subsequent frames until the next key frame—a process known as *frame differencing*. Although compression reduces video data significantly, there are still trade-offs involved without the use of additional high-powered hardware—trade-offs in image quality, image size, and frame rate.

Digital Video Standards

In the early days of multimedia, the processing requirements of digital video mandated pricey, dedicated hardware such as that used with Intel's DVI for both acquisition and playback. Apple's QuickTime broke the mold with the first digital video standard that required no additional hardware. An extension of the operating system, QuickTime was followed quickly by Microsoft's Video for Windows (and a video extension for OS/2), and Apple's QuickTime for Windows. Each is extensible, in that new *codecs* (compressors/decompressors) can be added that are designed for specific types of video, animation, and still image considerations. (Intel's Indeo codec was recently added to Video for Windows, for example.) These software-only solutions brought video capabilities to everyday computers and served as a major catalyst for the multimedia industry. (Codecs can also be added that support hardware-assisted compression for increased performance.)

Software-only video decompression served as catalyst

Digital video technologies must address issues not only of compression, but timing and synchronization—especially given the throughput disparities between various computers. One second of video must still take one second to play back. Moreover, audio and video must remain in sync in order for movies to avoid the dreaded bad lip-sync effect of dubbed films. As a solution, most software-only digital video standards are scalable— meaning that playback is optimized on the fly for the playback machine's throughput capabilities. The other option is hardware decompression circuitry that can play digital video at known parameters.

Most digital video technologies are scalable

The most entrenched video codecs are based on some form of *motion-JPEG*—proprietary expansions on the JPEG technology used with photorealistic still images. Motion-JPEG methods in technologies such as QuickTime and Video for Windows rely on the aforementioned trade-offs in image quality, image size, and frame rate. Image quality is usually set during production using the same concept of spatial compression ratios found in still-image JPEG. Image size can also be adjusted during production. Frame rate is usually adjusted automatically during playback. A typical software-only playback format is 320×240 pixels (one-quarter of an average screen) with moderate image quality at between 15 and 30 fps. This variation is because motion appears choppy at around 16 fps and individual images are perceived below about 12 fps.

Motion-JPEG is a popular compression solution

*Frames are dropped
during playback for
synchronization*

With motion-JPEG codecs under QuickTime, for example, the producer creates a video file at a specific compression quality, image size, and the maximum frame rate (see Figure 6.2). On playback, the delivery system prioritizes the audio and displays only the number of frames that it can display in the required period of time, ignoring the others. (One second's worth of video still transpires in one second, it's just that some of the information is missing.) At around 16 fps and lower, the jerky effect caused by the missing frames can result in perceived synchronization problems with the audio track such as poor lip sync. Some software and hardware schemes also facilitate *pixel doubling* in order to fill the screen without adding to the data stream. While pixel doubling makes it easier to see the video from a distance, image quality appears blocky on closer inspection.

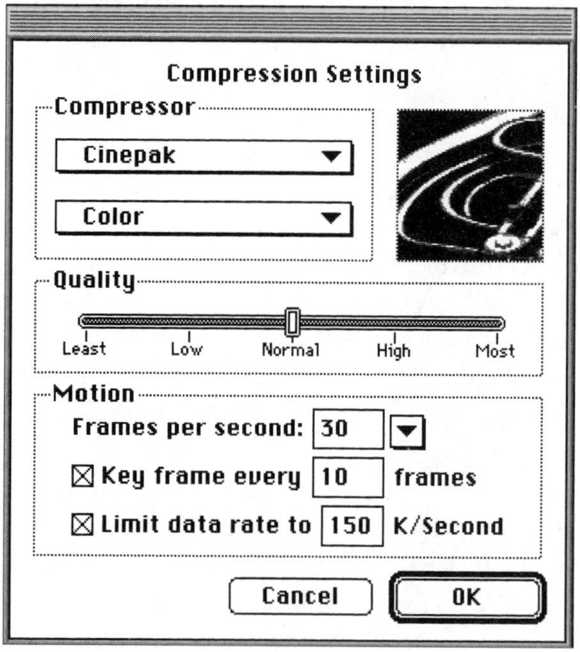

**FIGURE 6.2
A typical
QuickTime
compression
dialog box**

*Full-fidelity video is
available via hardware
decompression*

The trade-offs of image quality, size, and frame rate can be reduced or obviated through the use of hardware decompression (assuming that the added fidelity is present in the video file). While the price/performance ratio of decompression hardware is improving rapidly, there are still many variations on a theme. Over the next few years, we will see an increasing number of multimedia computers that have some form of hardware compression and matching decompression built in. It is only through this type of matched high-end hardware compression and decompression that uncompromised full-screen, full-fidelity, full-motion digital video is available directly from the computer.

The other popular compression technology is MPEG (Motion Picture Experts Group); it currently relies implicitly on hardware for full-screen, full-fidelity playback. MPEG-1 is designed for computer-based CD-ROM applications, T1 phone lines, and limited-traffic network use. MPEG-2 represents the evolution of MPEG-1 in that it looks better at significantly lower data rates—better facilitating the throughput required for multiple programs on cable and corporate networks. (MPEG-2 is also more flexible in accommodating other formats such as HDTV.) MPEG was conceived from inception to address the issues of motion. For starters, it employs temporal compression by recording only the differences between frames. It can also encode a panned camera movement across a background much more efficiently than motion-JPEG can. Reliance on special hardware decompression makes it possible for MPEG to be locked in at 30 fps, and image quality is determined during compression.

MPEG offers better efficiency and quality potential

Although MPEG can deliver better quality video than motion-JPEG, it has several comparative drawbacks. First, MPEG's implementation of frame differencing is so extensive that frame-accurate editing is cumbersome at best. (Where motion-JPEG can be frame accurate, MPEG must be decompressed in order to access individual frames.) Second, MPEG is highly asymmetric—meaning that compression is extremely processing-intensive in order to yield a data stream that can be decompressed in real time on playback. While six-figure mainframes were required for MPEG compression until recently, new Video RISC chip technology from C-Cube has lowered the bar to about $15,000 on desktop computers at this writing. In short, MPEG requires a much more serious commitment to digital video than technologies based on motion-JPEG. We're likely to see more use of MPEG in mass-market products such as Hollywood productions than in everyday business communication.

MPEG is more costly to produce

Video Hardware

Video Encoders

Video encoders convert to standard signals

The differences between video and computer signals reveal why you can't just plug a VCR into most computers and record an animation or presentation. A video encoder is required to convert the computer's RGB signal to NTSC or other traditional video format. Encoders can take the form of peripherals or can be built into video decompression circuitry.

Inexpensive video encoders don't provide broadcast quality

Encoders must address the issues of interlace and overscan, and their effectiveness in doing so is typically a function of price. Inexpensive encoders in the $400 range typically either place the image in a black border as on the computer screen or scale the image to fill the overscanned area—the latter potentially hiding some important image information. They also often cut corners by displaying only one of the interlaced fields and doubling each line. Better converters costing several thousand dollars display both fields, but often don't address issues such as flicker when single-pixel horizontal lines are displayed. Better products soften this problem and provide greater control over color balancing.

Important projects merit high-end conversion

Projects designed to be output to high-end video decks and/or broadcast require top-flight conversion. This is often accomplished by renting time on a high-end (around $25,000) scan converter in a video studio. Most of these devices can soften or eliminate flicker, control the degree of overscan, adjust color fidelity, zoom in on particular screen areas, accept a variety of computer sync signals, output component video and, in general, act as a visual Swiss Army Knife for conversions.

Video Digitizers and Playback Boards

Video digitizers incorporate hardware compression and decompression

During production, video is captured in the computer via a *video digitizer,* either in the form of add-in cards or dedicated circuitry found on some newer computers such as the Macintosh AV series. The capabilities of this input stage—both in terms of processing power and A-to-D component quality—determine the trade-offs inherent in the resulting master video file. You can get basic low-bandwidth video into the computer for under

$400 with products such as the VideoSpigot. Cards supporting anything close to full fidelity require dedicated hardware compression chips. Most of these include matching hardware decompression chips. The combination can boost the price to several thousand dollars—higher if the product includes a computer display adapter.

When evaluating video digitizers and playback cards, a bit of "specsmanship" is in order. Sixty fields per second (2 interlaced fields per second) is optimal; products supporting only 30 frames discard half the video information resulting in a potential loss in both fidelity and smoothness. Spatial resolution of 640 × 480 is required to fill the standard computer screen without pixel doubling and the associated artifacting. While some products only support 8-bit color, at least 15-bit color is necessary to approximate the potential color palette of video. Some manufacturers imply that their products can perform optimally in all of these areas, while far fewer actually perform to those specs simultaneously!

Quality is determined by a number of parameters

The types of inputs and outputs can also affect price and performance. Some cards accept only NTSC signals, while others support PAL and SECAM for international work. Most accept S-video input for cleaner signals. Only about half the cards currently on the market digitize audio— essential if you'll be digitizing footage that includes synchronized audio such as interviews or musical performances. As with sound cards, audio fidelity specs vary as well. The ability to pass audio through while digitizing also makes it possible to monitor sound while digitizing. Similar considerations are appropriate on cards supporting decompression. Not all provide the built-in or optional video encoding for NTSC (not to mention S-video, PAL, and SECAM) that is essential for output to tape.

Video input and output are important considerations

The bottom line is that video input and output hardware purchase decisions should be based on application. Many multimedia productions don't require full-screen video. Applications such as training, for example, may need only enough size and fidelity to get the point across. On the other hand, productions that will be viewed by the public, clients, and prospects (or output to videotape) require results of higher quality. How much higher will be determined by the situation and budget.

Match the technology to the application

MPEG popularity will increase as prices fall

As this book goes to press, several manufacturers are introducing MPEG playback boards for under $1,000. While the video performance of these cards is impressive, the primary application initially is viewing mass-market titles. Business usage will increase as the cost of MPEG compression and mastering goes down, eventually replacing laserdisc as a high-fidelity solution for training and other applications. In the interim, video post-production facilities that have invested in MPEG encoding provide a potentially cost-effective alternative to making the investment in-house.

Desktop Video Editors

Analog video editors control video decks

Computers have been instrumental in bringing pro and semi-pro video editing to the desktop. Products fall into the basic categories of analog and digital. *Analog video editors* are primarily software packages designed to control the transports of traditional video decks using established communications protocols. Footage is located, time code identifying in and out points for clips is captured, and EDLs (edit decision lists) are built that can control the source and record decks in editing a master tape. Some packages can also utilize video digitizers to acquire thumbnail videos facilitating visual editing of clip in and out points, which then generate the EDL. Better packages allow the thumbnails to be placed in tracks on a timeline for a more visually intuitive interface.

Digital video editors are nonlinear

Digital or *nonlinear video editors* exclusively manipulate digitized video. They take the form of either dedicated turnkey systems ($4,000 to $40,000) or combinations of video compression/decompression hardware with video encoders and compatible digital video editing software. Clips are digitized to hard disk, in and out points are visually selected, and the clips are typically placed in tracks along a timeline. Transitions, graphics, text, overlays and special effects can be added and the results are rendered into a new digital video file in the format of choice. The massive storage and throughput issues associated with sophisticated digital video typically require investing in a disk array—multiple hard drives working in concert to significantly reduce sustained transfer rates.

Analog and digital editors offer trade-offs

Both types of systems have their pluses and minuses. Analog tape costs about $.10 per minute, while each minute of digital usurps about $100 worth of hard disk space. In addition to a master record deck, analog requires a separate playback deck for each simultaneously viewed layer of video (including overlapping segments during transitions). Digital can use a single deck to input an unlimited number of tracks and record the final output, although time must be budgeted to digitize the footage. Analog requires a switcher for transitions and DVE (digital video effects) for fancy stuff like spin-flipping video windows (see Figure 6.3). While these effects can be performed digitally in software, they require rendering time in current desktop systems. Similarly, analog editing requires lots of time-consuming tape shuttling that can degrade the tapes, while complex passages on digital can take plenty of time to render.

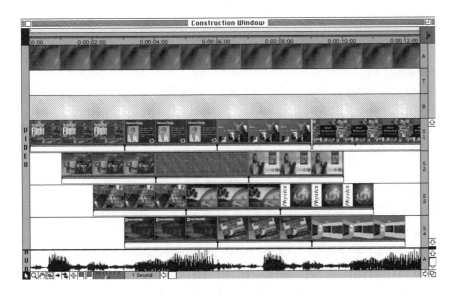

FIGURE 6.3
Digital video editing with Adobe Premiere

Traditional video production has spawned the concept of off-line versus on-line editing. *Off-line editing* performs rough edits on tape copies using inexpensive equipment to establish timing and edit points for the subsequent *on-line editing* session utilizing the original footage in a full-blown, full-price studio. Desktop tools modify this paradigm in several ways. First, editing with digital video at the off-line stage enables much better visualization of effects (and at a lower cost) than most tape-based corollaries. Moreover, nonlinear editing permits easy "what if" experiments in an on-line environment that would normally only be cost effective off-line. Finally, off-line work can often be converted to on-line finals by substituting

Desktop tools blur lines between off-line and on-line editing

full-resolution footage for work proxies. (Digitizing full-fidelity video footage of any length can be a time-consuming proposition. Service bureaus are beginning to appear to handle this specialized need.)

Frame Controllers

Individual frames of 3-D animation are recorded to video

While a common use of 3-D software is to render a series of high-res 24-bit animation frames, few desktop computers have the throughput necessary to display these sequences in real time. The solution is the use of a *frame controller* to control a frame-accurate video deck. The software loads a frame from hard disk, prerolls the video deck, records a single frame, pauses the deck, then repeats the process for the entire series of frames. While this process is potentially time consuming, some software can make a pass that records every *nth* frame according to how fast the frames can be loaded from disk, then make another pass recording every *nth*+1 frame and so forth until all the frames are filled in. Software-only solutions sell for about $500 while hardware versions run several thousand dollars.

Video Servers

Video servers bring real-time video to networks

Multimedia's move from stand-alone computers to networked computing is being facilitated by *video servers*—specialized types of file servers that typically impose isochronous protocols on existing LANs. In order to support network delivery of video, the server must have considerable processing power and bus bandwidth, and the network itself must utilize a streaming protocol and have significant bandwidth. Starlight Networks' Media Server, for example, currently turns a 50 mHz 486 PC with RAID disk arrays into a sort of video PBX system capable of supporting 20 simultaneous users on a standard Novell network. Multiple users can access the same video simultaneously and hundreds of users can be supported with switched hubs in an enterprise network (see Figure 6.4). Systems based on the SGI platform are being used in test markets of interactive cable. Video server technology is still in its infancy and will grow tremendously as network bandwidths improve and the information superhighway evolves.

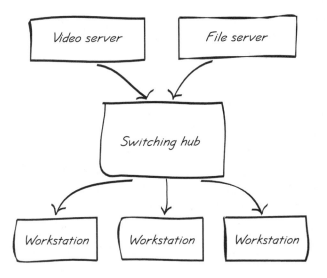

FIGURE 6.4
Video servers typically work in conjunction with traditional file servers

Other Video Tools

As with audio, professional video studios utilize many different compo-nents, some of which come into play with more sophisticated desktop productions. While the details are beyond the scope of this book, video cameras and decks come in a variety of formats. In general, VHS and 8mm should be used only as a delivery medium. Industrial projects should be shot on a minimum of S-VHS, Hi-8 or 3/4" due to their higher reso-lution and fidelity. Serious productions should employ Betacam SP, 1" or similar professional format.

Choice of format affects quality

Laserdiscs employ optical disk technology similar to CD-ROMs, but are dedicated to encoding as much as one hour of analog video per side. Laserdisc players (currently $1,000 to $2,000) were once the choice delivery medium for video in multimedia, owing to their high quality, random access, and computer control. They have largely been replaced by less costly, integrated, digital solutions such as motion-SPEG and MPEG. Laserdiscs require a mastering process typically performed by video production facilities using laserdisc recorders. Laserdisc recorders (approximately $12,000) are sometimes also used in multimedia produc-tion to record long sequences of 3–D rendered animation frames for video that would be prohibitive to store as digital data.

Laserdisc use is diminishing

Many other tools come into play in complete video studios

Serious video work should also utilize lighting and professional micro-phones. Other studio components include switchers for live mixing of video signals, DVEs for effects such as video within video and spin flips, character generators for fast video titling, and waveform monitor and vec-torscopes for signal optimization, TBCs (time-base correctors) for synchronizing several source signals, and much more. (All of these are dis-cussed in greater depth in *The Desktop Multimedia Bible*.) Many of these tools are available in desktop, semi-pro, and industrial formats and/or are available for rent. One tool of particular note is Newtek's Video Toaster, which combines a switcher, DVE, character generator, 3-D animation environment, and more into an Amiga-compatible board for under $2,500. Indeed, in a world dominated by PC and Mac, the Toaster pro-vides a compelling reason to dedicate an Amiga to this aspect of video production.

Video Software

Video software primarily falls in the categories of editing, special effects, and stock footage.

Editing

Video editors serve as controllers or nonlinear editors

Video editing software has already been touched on in light of video edit-ing systems. Products like Gold Disk's Video Director are designed primarily to control video decks during logging and editing. Packages like Adobe Premiere are aimed at nonlinear editing of digital video on hard disks using compression such as QuickTime and AVI in conjunction with hardware compression cards and optional decompression cards. These tools typically provide for multiple video and audio tracks, transitions, some effects, EDL, and deck control at around $500.

Special Effects

Some packages add special effects not found in basic editing tools

As Hollywood continues to invent new special effects, the multimedia industry strives to bring them to the desktop. Packages like CoSA After Effects and VideoFusion focus less on editing and more on superimposition, flying windows, and filter effects that change over time. *Morphing*—the ability to seamlessly transform one image into another over time popular-ized by movies like *Terminator 2* and countless commercials—is available for under $100 in products like Gryphon's Morph and HSC's Digital Morph (see Figure 6.5). The results of these packages can be integrated into digital editing packages.

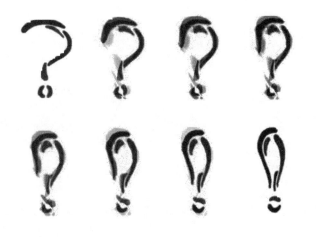

**FIGURE 6.5
A morphing
sequence**

Stock Footage

As with stock photography, stock footage libraries provide producers with a wealth of licensed imagery that would be prohibitive (if not impossible) to shoot themselves. Licensing fees vary between stock houses, but you can definitely expect to pay much more for big-name productions. Most TV networks now license historical news footage at moderate prices. Many other companies specialize in specific types of footage like vintage, aviation, nature, travel, and so forth. A good source for these companies is the back of video and television production magazines such as *Post* and *Millimeter*, or Hollywood source books.

Stock film libraries can save time and money

7

Media Integration and Delivery

Delivery Hardware

There are many vehicles for delivering multimedia. The components you choose will depend upon the project.

CD-ROM Players

CD-ROM technology was described in depth in Chapter 3. There are a handful of decisions to be made when purchasing CD-ROM players. The first is whether to purchase a CD-ROM alone (around $200 to $300) or, in the case of the PC, spend about twice the money on a multimedia upgrade kit that includes a CD-ROM drive. For PCs that don't already have a sound card, the latter is recommended in order to minimize installation headaches and conflicts. When choosing players alone, the choice of internal or external models will be partially influenced by the internal space available in your chassis. Internal models often have the ability to connect directly to the internal sound system or sound card, eliminating external connections and sometimes providing a digital pathway from CD audio output to internal recording and mixing circuitry. While most external models use SCSI (small computer serial interface), internal models typically come with a choice of bus types to match a given system. (SCSI is a worthwhile investment that facilitates expansion and flexibility.)

There are several configuration choices

As for speed, a minimum of double speed (approximately 300KB transfer rate) is highly recommended. Compressed video will run more smoothly and animation will play faster on faster drives. In general, buy all the speed you can afford, realizing that prices are lowering on given speed drives as faster models become available. Many of the faster drives include a RAM buffer to enhance smooth thoughput. It is also advisable to purchase drives that can read multisession discs and are shipped with drivers for protocols such as ISO 9660 and Kodak Photo CD.

Speed and format are important factors

CD-ROM Recorders

*The price/
performance ratio of
CD-ROM recorders
is improving*

CD-ROM recorders are plummeting in price, with systems that sold for $20,000 a few years ago selling for under $8,000 complete with software. The mechanism itself is pretty straightforward. As with CD-ROM drives, speed is important since a single-speed unit can take between 60 and 90 minutes to write a complete 650MB CD-ROM. Double-speed and faster recorders are beginning to appear, although with a price difference. Not all models are multisession capable (appending new information to old recordings), an important feature when dealing with data that requires frequent updating. Some units come with built-in hard drives, a bonus since many packages require disk space to make virtual images on disk before actually writing the CD. (In situations without built-in drives, plan to dedicate a hard disk of at least 670MB, since constantly reformatting partitions on a larger drive can be tedious.)

*Software determines a
great deal of recording
performance*

Software is by far more important to purchase decisions than the hardware. Most CD-ROM recorders are bundled with software and, though there's some ability to mix and match, not all software works with all hardware. Some packages only record the host's native file hierarchy, while better offerings can record ISO, Red Book audio, and other file structures. Software can also influence the amount of time it takes to write to the CD. The aforementioned process where some software creates a virtual image on disk usually adds more time to the recording process than direct writes. Not mutually exclusive, however, is the ability to reduce record time by writing only selected files and folders or adjusting the size of the overall data image to be less than the full 650MB.

Laptop LCD Displays

*Active matrix LCD
is required for
dynamic delivery*

Laptop computers with color LCDs (liquid crystal displays) provide a great method of creating and delivering presentations virtually anywhere. There are basically two types of LCD screens—passive and active matrix. While *passive matrix* screens can be used for basic presentations, they are too slow for elements such as animation, video, and flashy transitions. *Active matrix* screens are critical for the delivery of dynamic presentations. Note that most active matrix screens built into laptops are still too slow to display full-motion video.

Projection Systems

There are a wide range of projection systems available for various size venues. Companies who do a handful of major shows per year usually rent projection systems from local A-V rental houses. Most of these units have either front- or rear-projection systems, with a single lens or a separate lens for each RGB color. The former is typically more portable and requires less tedious setup and convergence than the latter. Many A-V companies employ two identical projectors focused in tandem to double the illumination—a technique that makes convergence significantly more difficult.

RGB projectors can be difficult to transport and set up

Color active-matrix LCD technology has made projection for small- to mid-sized rooms simpler and more portable. LCD panels small enough to fit in a briefcase have recently come down in price (around $5,000 to $7,000) and have increased in fidelity. Several sizes are available, with the larger ones translating to greater projected image size. The biggest problem with these panels is that they rely on overhead projectors. These typically exhibit a keystoning (tapered) effect in the projected image—although some LCDs actually have circuitry to compensate for this. They also require a projector with metal-halide bulbs sporting 3,000 to 4,000 lumens of light in order to yield optimal brightness, contrast, and color. (There are plenty of tired old overhead projectors lurking about, so it's best to verify exact specs when going on location or bring your own projector. Several manufacturers now offer portable self-contained LCD projectors that offer easy setup, required illumination, and more predictable results at prices ranging between $7,500 and $13,000.

Self-contained LCD projectors offer portability and fidelity

Feature sets in both LCD panels and projectors are similar. Better units attain better fidelity through higher contrast ratios. (60:1 ratios represent the low end of the scale, and 200:1 ratios currently represent about the best.) Color depths range from 256,000 to 16.7 million. Even with active-matrix LCDs, faster response times will ensure greater smoothness with full-motion video sources. Compatibility and switching between as many computer and video input sources as possible will provide the greatest flexibility, as does pass-through to other types of output. Other feature possibilities include computer-video overlay, zoom, built-in speakers, remote controls, cases, and pointers that serve as remote mice.

Evaluate features in context of your needs

Media Integration Software

Match the right tool to the job

Media integration software packages are ultimately the tools by which various media components are brought together into a structure and flow. The field is loosely divided into presentation packages, tools for creating larger-scale dynamic productions, and authoring tools for interactive training and education. While the lines continue to blur between the feature sets of these genres, the key in evaluating the plethora of packages out there is matching the right tool for the job. This is true not only with regard to features, but with ease of use for novices.

Screen metaphor and compatibility differ between packages

Most media integration tools employ one of the following screen metaphors: movie screen, slide show, a group of screens linked together, a stack of similar cards, or actors on a stage. Similarly, the development interface typically takes one of these forms: a list of media events, iconic flowchart, card stack, linked objects, a series of frames, or scripting language. Regardless of the genre, one of the criteria in choosing any media integration package is delivery options. Any need for cross-platform compatibility (typically between Mac and PC) will limit the choices to software that has either a complete development counterpart on each system or can export a file for a non-native run-time player.

Presentation Software

Presentation packages emulate the slide projector

The main focus of *presentation software* is enabling novices to create and deliver business presentations in the mold of the slide show. Most packages employ the metaphor of a slide projector. They typically include text outliners and may import outlines from other business packages. Each major heading signals the beginning of a new slide. Templates are used to determine how the heads and subheads are formatted and displayed over backgrounds, including attributes such as position, size, font, style, and color. Some presentation packages have basic drawing tools. Most also print hidden speaker notes or audience handouts. Presentation packages such as Aldus Persuasion and Gold Disk Astound (see Figure 7.1) typically run between $300 and $500.

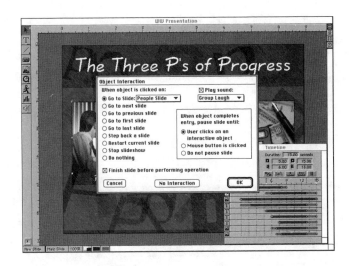

FIGURE 7.1
Gold Disk
Astound's
presentation
interface

For more ambitious presentations, many packages now also include support for dynamic media such as audio, video, and animation—usually in the form of imported elements. Path-based animation allows text and other graphic elements to fly into position or across the screen. Interactivity is typically limited to *simple branching* where on-screen buttons or hot spots are programmed to navigate to specific points in response to mouse clicks.

Most software supports dynamic media and interactivity

Production Software

Production software is typically oriented toward producing content that is more ambitious than the slide-show level. Packages usually integrate all types of multimedia data into a multitrack timeline that determines the evolution of events. Productions that rely heavily on synchronization often benefit from packages like Passport Producer that are based on SMPTE (Society of Motion Picture and Television Engineers) or other absolute time standard. Packages like Macromedia Director also facilitate the internal creation of animation (see Figure 7.2). Interactivity usually takes the form of the more sophisticated *conditional branching* that can make navigation decisions based on user input and other conditions. Better packages support other forms of user input such as keyboard entry of data, scrolling of text, and video playback control. Many products in this category also support device control for hardware such as laserdisc players. Production software is typically designed for the more advanced user and most offerings are priced between $400 and $1,200.

Production software creates dynamic content

FIGURE 7.2
Macromedia
Director's
production
interface

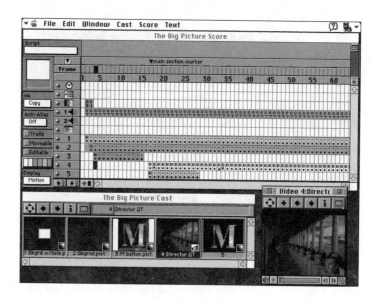

Authoring Software

Authoring software is used in training and education

Authoring software is primarily designed to create education or training content. One popular metaphor is the card stack found in Apple's Hypercard or Asymetrix's Multimedia Toolbook, designed primarily to present information conforming to the model of an interactive book. The other popular metaphor found in products like AimTech's Icon Author and Macromedia's Authorware (see Figure 7.3) is the icon-based flow-chart. The latter typically supports superior user input, testing, logic for remedial review, conditional branching, device control, and test printouts. Like production software, authoring packages typically require a significant commitment in structuring a complete project. This area of specialization usually incurs price tags around the $5,000 mark.

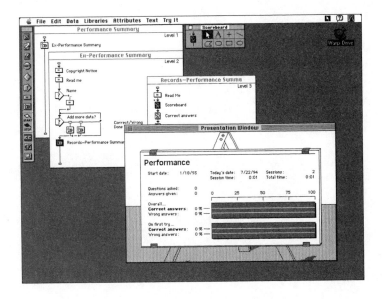

FIGURE 7.3
Macromedia Authorware's authoring interface

Multimedia-oriented programming languages such as Visual Basic represent another authoring alternative. While potentially more difficult to master than packages with graphical user interfaces, this approach potentially offers the greatest flexibility, performance speed, and power. Kaleida Labs' ScriptX is an authoring language designed specifically for high-performance, cross-platform delivery of multimedia. Some content developers also create their own authoring environments to avoid the shortcomings of off-the-shelf tools.

Programming languages represent power tools

8

Investment Decisions and Preliminaries

The way in which you approach the implementation of multimedia production depends on factors such as how often multimedia will be used, how sophisticated those productions will be, in-house talent and equipment, and overall budgeting. This chapter is designed to offer insight into the choices surrounding the production vehicle.

Address the needs of your organization

Investment Decisions

Aside from the obvious mandate of cost effectiveness, the two main factors to consider when establishing a production system are quality and efficiency. Both concepts can be applied to equipment and human resources.

Quality and efficiency are the two main issues

The Importance of Aesthetics

With all the hype about desktop tools, one of the most overlooked aspects of multimedia is aesthetics. As put forth in the introduction, the most powerful of tools won't produce satisfactory results without a modicum of talent and experience. This is not to say that compelling do-it-yourself presentations are not possible by novices. In my experience, the greatest requisite is the acknowledgment that aesthetics are important, the possession of some basic creative ability, and the desire to learn. Most people, for example, can learn the tenets of good design and hone their implementation of those principles over time.

Recognize that aesthetics are important

The more important the production, the more sophisticated its aesthetic needs become. A presentation to in-house staff, for example, doesn't necessarily require a great deal of production value. By contrast, a production aimed at selling a product or service to others requires greater pizzazz and attention to detail. Regardless of your audience, our society on the whole has become accustomed to the multimillion dollar sights and sounds of mainstream media. The second we see something with motion and sound

The importance of aesthetics increases with that of the message

on a monitor, it is subconsciously judged against Hollywood, Madison Avenue, and MTV. If the message is worth presenting and you want the audience to retain it, some degree of attention to aesthetics is in order.

Using Existing Resources

Do-it-yourself slide shows are typical candidates

Basic business presentations that follow the slide-show model demand the least time, talent, and equipment to produce. Given simple software, templates, clip media, and a little knowledge of design principles, most people delivering the message are capable of creating the necessary presentation themselves. Many businesses have a color scanner and accompanying image editing software that can be used to digitize photos, brochures, and similar custom elements.

Communication and art departments can share the load

If your company has a corporate communications department, their existing resources may be able to help with structuring the message, as well as providing access to existing media. An in-house graphics or desktop publishing team can most likely provide visual elements in electronic form such as logos, charts, and product shots. They are also likely candidates for overall implementation of the presentation—and may even be capable of animating some of the graphic elements.

In-house video departments can help with dynamic productions

More ambitious productions bring a greater need for specialists, both to create component pieces of the media puzzle and to integrate them. Here, an in-house graphics department may or may not feel comfortable making the leap from print to screen if a lot of animation, 3-D, or special effects are required. Integrating sound and motion is more akin to video production than print production—both in terms of discipline and technical orientation. If your company has an in-house video department, chances are good that they will have the skill and interest to make the leap to the digital video you may wish to incorporate in multimedia productions.

Expanding Internal Resources versus Outsourcing

Needs analysis is the first step

Reliance on existing resources begs the question of whether these departments have the additional time to take on multimedia or are already working to (or beyond) capacity. Moreover, the equipment used for traditional print and video production may not be up to the task of ambitious multimedia production. The first order of business is needs analysis. First, determine how many productions your company will require or benefit from over a given period of time. Second, establish how sophisticated they will need to be. Next, visualize the various job descriptions required for that level of sophistication—producer, writer, videographer/editor, composer/engineer, designer, artist, animator, and programmer being typical job descriptions. (The use of stock media can eliminate some of these creative needs.) Simultaneously, evaluate the amount of equipment required to do each of these jobs at the expected quality level.

Three logical alternatives present themselves. The first is to grow the production team and purchase enough equipment for effective productivity. While costs will vary with expectations and scale, the issue of return on investment mandates a constant flow of production work. Similarly, the rapid pace at which technology becomes obsolete mandates carefully choosing equipment that will pay for itself before the wheels of progress march right over it. The investment in equipment and human skills is easier to justify if it represents an expansion or crossover with existing creative services departments.

An in-house production team can require a large investment

The opposite extreme is to outsource all productions to an independent production company or producer who will assemble a team. This approach has the benefit of eliminating the permanent overhead of equipment and production staff. Each production will typically cost more than the hours of labor associated with in-house production, simply because production companies must pay for their equipment investment and production time (as well as their own marketing efforts and meeting time required to negotiate contracts and establish a wavelength about your needs). In the final analysis, you also lose some control when contracting outside creative services. While large corporations are often more comfortable doing business with other large companies, most multimedia production companies are small. Moreover, independent producers such as myself embrace the movie studio paradigm of assembling the best team for each project.

Outsourcing eliminates equipment and human resource issues

The third alternative is a hybrid where a core in-house team outsources pieces of the multimedia puzzle as necessary. Many companies feel that this yields the best of both worlds. A staff producer would be familiar with the company's message, style, budget, and internal politics while

An in-house core supplemented by outside services is a popular solution

acting in the employer's best interest. Such a producer can supplement internal resources from any art, video, and communication departments with the skills of selected freelance specialists and service bureaus. (Video production and original music are primary candidates for outsourcing.) This in some ways follows the model of a magazine or ad agency where the staff creative director hires the right talent according to the needs of each specific project—most of whom have invested in their own equipment. Equipment can also be rented on a short-term basis in order to fulfill a given project. The in-house equipment requirements vary with each scenario, but are invariably much more modest than gearing up a complete facility.

Preliminaries: Concept, Budget, and Timetable

Concept development is the first task

As with everything in life, a multimedia project begins with a concept—one typically driven by need. That concept must be developed beyond a simple idea in order to make real progress in budgeting, scheduling, and other areas. Even if you have moderate in-house production capabilities, fleshing out the concept will determine if you need the assistance of outside production services for some or all of the job. Try writing down a synopsis of the idea, describing the catalyst, goals, and what you see in your mind's eye. This can either be in paragraph form, outline form, or both. This step will help solidify your own thinking and provide something tangible to communicate to others. This is the initial step toward the invaluable storyboarding process described in Chapter 9.

Establish a timeline

Next, establish a basic timeline in which the project must be completed, and milestones along the way at which any known pieces of the puzzle will be available. At this stage those puzzle pieces may be as simple as a meeting at which a marketing plan, product feature set, or marketing budget may be solidified—or they may be as detailed as dates when logos, copy, related brochures, or videos are completed. This too will help provide a reality check as to feasibility and give others a better picture.

Budgeting

Beyond a do-it-yourself presentation, budgeting for in-house production is largely an issue of human labor and the system your company uses for internal costing. Nonetheless, hard dollars may also come into play in purchasing or renting equipment, obtaining stock images and footage, and contracting freelancers or service bureaus for elements exceeding the capabilities of in-house resources. (The concept treatment and timelines will be very valuable in conferring with associates).

Establish a budget

If the project warrants outsourcing the entire production, the concept and timelines will be invaluable in getting on a wavelength with a multimedia producer. Don't feel awkward if you don't know what multimedia costs. It's the same answer as to the question of how much video production costs—anywhere from $100 to $10,000 a finished minute and even beyond, depending on whether you're talking camcorders or a Hollywood studio!

Multimedia costs cover quite a range

Conversely, producers are used to all manner of projects large and small, not to mention plenty of tire kickers. Their natural response to the question of how much it costs is "how much do you want to spend." Since most people are uncomfortable with answering this question up front, it once again pays to be able to paint as complete a picture about your concept and timeline as possible. At some point, it's going to come down to establishing if you're both in the same monetary ballpark, so it's prudent to have examined the minimum and maximum you're willing to spend. Quotes are often framed according to levels of sophistication, giving the client several options.

Accurate expectations are the key to fixing a budget

In all candor, multimedia producers aren't going to get rich from your project. Most media production is highly competitive, the hours are long, the skills are specialized, the learning curve is ongoing, and the pace of technology makes equipment obsolete all too quickly. Producers also want your repeat business. As with any industry, doing continued good business is often preferable to the cost and effort of advertising, prospecting, and courting new clients. Most people in multimedia are in it because they just want to do what they love—not because they need a wheelbarrow to go to the bank! (They're usually also looking to do quality projects to update their demo reels.)

Few producers are in it for the money

The result of all this is that you typically wind up exchanging ranges of figures with a producer and continuing to narrow it down to a more finite number if you're both in the same ballpark. In this exchange the need for more detail increases. Presented here is my Production Visualization Questions list borrowed from *The Desktop Multimedia Bible*. Combined with a friendly drink, it is the most effective vehicle I've found to establishing enough of a wavelength to firm up a bid.

Production Visualization Questions

- What is the purpose of the production?
- How will the success of the production be measured?
- Who is the audience—professionally, demographically, and psychologically?
- What is the proposed length of the production?
- How will the production be delivered?
- What are the circumstances under which the production will be viewed?
- What is the balance of information detail versus excitement level?
- What is the desired action on the part of the audience?
- What is the audience's current attitude toward the subject?
- What problems does the production or its subject solve for the viewer?
- What are the main three to five points of the message in order of importance?
- What is the subliminal message or benefit?
- What should the product or subject feel, look, and sound like stylistically to the viewer?
- What should be the overall pace?
- How much motion will be effective? Will the product need to move? Will the viewer's perspective need to move?
- Do any overall stylistic treatments come to mind such as drama, nostalgia, science fiction, mystery, or parody?

continued

---

continued

- What image is to be portrayed about the company, product, or subject?
- Do any existing materials, styles, and themes (such as logos, slogans, artwork, ads, photos, videos, and brochures) need to be carried over for continuity and synergy?
- Do any usable source materials exist, especially in electronic form?
- Do elements of this production need to be carried over into other projects?
- What production elements—video, animation, 3D, music, and so forth—are envisioned?
- Is the use of any particular platform, hardware, or software mandated?
- What is the production and delivery timetable—including performance and payment milestones?
- Assuming one gets what one pays for, what are the minimum and maximum amounts of money that can be budgeted for the project?
- Who has the authority to sign off on ideas, budgets, and schedules?

Trade-Offs

You've no doubt heard the service industry adage that given price, quality, and time, you can have any two. In this regard, multimedia is no different than printing, video, or any other creative service you may be accustomed to. Nobody wants to compromise quality and time seems to be a fading commodity—leaving money. In contracting outside services, rush charges often legitimately go directly to pay for the additional people and equipment to meet a tight deadline from that end. Even if the production is to be done in-house, price must be measured in terms of not only equipment, but labor hours, and even potential employee burnout by pushing fixed resources too far. Given tight budgets, it's easy to go around in circles. (See Figure 8.1.)

The quintessential trade-offs are quality, price, and time

**FIGURE 8.1
Trade-offs in any
media production**

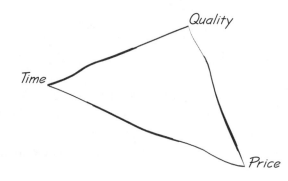

*Choose quality over
quantity*

A reality check is in order to solve the equation. If time and money are inflexible, then quality should be examined—not literally, but in terms of what you expect to integrate into the production. It's better to have a shorter production of high quality, for example, than to have a longer one of mediocre quality. Original music, graphics, and video typically cost more than clip media. (Licensing stock photography and library movie footage can also add up.) 3-D graphics usually costs more than 2-D. Motion typically costs more than static images and in-place transitions. In general, more flash costs more money.

Spreading the Wealth

*Amortize elements
across multiple
productions*

One way of keeping the costs down on a multimedia production is by using elements that already exist. Product photos, company videos, brochures, marketing copy, charts, and databases can often be culled as elements. Conversely, look at amortizing the investment you make across other company projects. Elements from multimedia production might be integrated into other marketing vehicles like brochures, trade-show displays, and videos. Similarly, other departments wanting to do multimedia productions of their own might be able to repurpose elements from the current project, or even reuse the whole thing with small modifications. A production element such as a photo might be used in related aspects of the project, such as handouts, ads, posters, videos, and so forth.

9

The Production Process

The proven phases of preproduction, production, and post-production established in the realization of tradition media apply to multimedia as well. While the lines sometimes blur between these stages with desktop production tools, an understanding of the basic functions of each phase will help clarify the overall production process (see Figure 9.1).

Projects include preproduction, production, and post-production

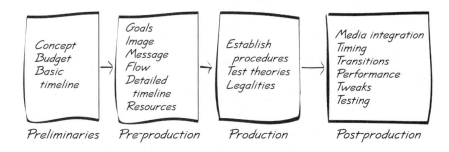

FIGURE 9.1
The stages of a classic production

Preproduction

Preproduction is essentially the planning phase of a project. As with anything, it's easier to get where you want to go if you have a destination and a map. In multimedia, proper planning can make the difference between success and failure with regard to schedule, budget, and effectiveness.

Preproduction is all-important

Establishing Goals

The most important thing in most multimedia presentations and productions—indeed, in any business communication—is establishing the message you wish the viewer or audience to retain. Distill the essence of what you want to say to a single, concise main point, no matter how complex the issue or how many features and angles there are. Equally important, clearly define the desired results in terms of the action you want the audience to take. Is this merely an image-building piece? Do you want them to buy something on the spot or find a sales outlet? Is this a catalyst for the next step in a process?

Determine the desired results at the outset

Contrast creativity with flexibility and reliability

Another measurement of goals is the project's ambition level in light of reliability and flexibility. Higher levels of creative aesthetics can make projects more difficult and costly to edit and later modify. As for reliability, a major production or kiosk installation requires a significant amount of testing in contrast to a small one-time presentation.

Establishing Image

Establish an audience profile

In order to frame and convey the message properly, a profile of the audience also needs to be established. Are they a captive audience? If so, there's a little more time to set the stage; if not, the message will have to hit hard and fast in order to prevent prospects from moving on.

Specific age groups dictate certain aesthetics

Demographics can also heavily influence the way in which the message is couched. At the risk of stereotyping, age groups can affect the style of the music, graphics, video, and narrative. Younger audiences, for instance, would respond to up-tempo hip-hop beats, wild graphics, fast music-video style edits, and modern slang. These would be poor choices indeed for a presentation on retirement communities to an elderly audience! Here, something more classy, subdued, jazzy, and nostalgic would be in order. Speaking of nostalgia, the sights and sounds of their youth can be used to pull at the heartstrings of the Baby Boom generation—tempered with the modern stylistic influences embodied in mainstream media such as TV, radio, and magazines.

Speak to the lifestyle of the audience

Income bracket, education, and lifestyle can be of similar influence with regard to the style of the media elements. Moreover, can audience members appreciate, use, and afford the package you're selling? Assuming that's not an issue, talk to them at their level and in the language of their peers. Present imagery that speaks to their lifestyle or business goal—or the one you want them to associate with the results of your product or service!

Gender represents another aesthetic

Gender can also play a major determining role in designing production aesthetics. Consider whether your audience will respond to more bold or laid-back music, brighter or softer colors, faster or slower pacing, and messages that are more aggressive or subtle.

There are many other ways in which to profile audiences. Nationalities have obvious imagery, color combinations, and ethnic music that can be used to hit home—especially given today's ethnic-marketing techniques. Geographic region, profession, political affiliation, interests, and creative/analytical orientation are just some of the other angles. Many times audiences won't fall uniformly into clearly defined pigeonholes across all categories. It is then advisable to take a middle-of-the-road stylistic approach to those parameters in hopes of avoiding offense and boredom on either extreme.

There are many other ways to categorize an audience

Once an image is targeted for the audience, it must be integrated with your image. If your corporate image is well established, this may require little thought or deviation. If a great deal of time and money has been expended embodying that image in print or other media, it may be best or even mandatory to perpetuate that style. If a new direction is desired, establish how you want the audience to perceive your company or product. Is it well established, or the new kid on the block? Where does it fall on the scale of conservative to hip? Should the image be one of button-down formality and power, or shirt-sleeves casual and light-hearted fun? An overtly humorous approach can be effective in some situations. There are, of course, many variations on these and other themes—all of which need to be considered along with the audience profile in arriving at an overall style.

Integrate the audience profile with your product

Crafting the Message

Establishing the major point, goal, audience profile, and company image provides criteria and context that can be used in crafting the message. Ideally, these guidelines can be used to create a metaphor or theme that you can integrate with the main message and then use as a thread to weave the various components of the production together. Such a theme would be introduced in the introduction as a title or slogan. Important points throughout can then be phrased to reinforce that metaphor. Scripts can be written that incorporate subtle references through clever plays on words. It may even be desirable to make things more interesting by framing the whole production in a dramatic style such as comedy, mystery, science fiction, or action. The importance of choosing or creating visuals and music to reinforce the theme cannot be overemphasized.

Develop a theme

Use words, imagery, and music that empower the audience

Conversely, such a theme can often provide ideas for graphics in situations where the product or service is not easily depicted. Given the right theme, this kind of nonliteral imagery can also serve to communicate a form of empowerment to the audience. The concept of empowering the audience reinforces that communicating with multimedia is no different from communicating with other media. The universal tenets of sales and marketing apply. Use proactive phrases like "it does," rather than "it can" or "it will." Examine whether you're selling the sizzle or the steak. Don't talk up or down to audiences, but instead as peers.

Restrict the number of points being made

Linear Production Flow   In fleshing out the body of the production, try to distill the *three* to *five main points* that are most important for the audience to walk away with—the fewer the better. It has been widely documented that pushing much past this number leaves an audience confused and retaining nothing. Weed out points that aren't critical. Frame the remaining elements of the message as subordinate points that reinforce the three main ones. Drive those main points home at every opportunity. Ideally, weave them in with the main thematic thread.

Use preview and review to drive points home

One effective approach in marketing messages is to proceed by establishing the state of the industry, the current *problem*, and the *solution* your company is introducing. This is followed by benefits, who will use the product or service in various real-world situations, and the closing call to action. You've probably heard the old adage, "tell them what you're going to tell them, then tell them, then tell them what you told them." Translated to the framework of linear multimedia production, this dictates a preview or agenda at the beginning and a review or summary at the end. If there are a considerable number of subpoints, it is often advisable to keep the audience oriented by providing minisummaries and a return to the overview between major points.

Perfect the script or storyboard first

Once the message and structure are established, the conceptual treatment can be transformed into an outline or script. In speaker-support type presentations, the outline is literally translated to the textual points displayed on the screen. In other productions, the outline serves as a stepping stone and checkpoint before going into the scripting process. Scripting should reflect any stylistic and thematic decisions that have been made. The finished script usually includes a storyboard or similar method of visualizing the audio-visual content that parallels each segment. A common practice is to break the page into three columns containing (1) a description of any sound and action, (2) a sketch or picture of what will be on the screen, and (3) the actual words to be delivered in the narration (see Figure 9.2).

**FIGURE 9.2
One type of storyboard layout**

Maintaining a steady volume level and speed is a sure path to putting an audience to sleep. Linear presentations of any length should therefore be dynamic in both regards. This might be done by structuring segments with clear breaks between. Longer segments could build gradually, shorter ones could switch to a different level of pacing altogether. Segments with

Employ dynamics to retain audience interest

lots of animation or video should be spaced out to spread the wealth. On the whole, momentum should increase while building to the finale. It is often useful to check or plan the dynamics by graphing them on a time-line (see Figure 9.3).

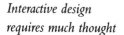

Interactive design requires much thought

Interactive Production Flow Interactive productions place more control over flow in the hands of the user. The degree to which this is permitted is still up to the producer. In the case of an information system such as an in-house multimedia database, flow is determined almost entirely by the user. In interactive training situations, the course usually proceeds in a clearly structured path and user interaction is largely used as a testing mechanism.

Interactivity can incorporate linear segments

In productions more oriented to marketing, the trick is to give the user enough freedom to pique interest and explore the subject, yet ensure that the important parts of the message are still presented. This can be accomplished by incorporating linear sequences into the interactive options. The production can open, for example, with a linear passage that incorporates the main message. Subsequent choices by the viewer can each lead to a passage presenting the requested information while underscoring related points (see Figure 9.4).

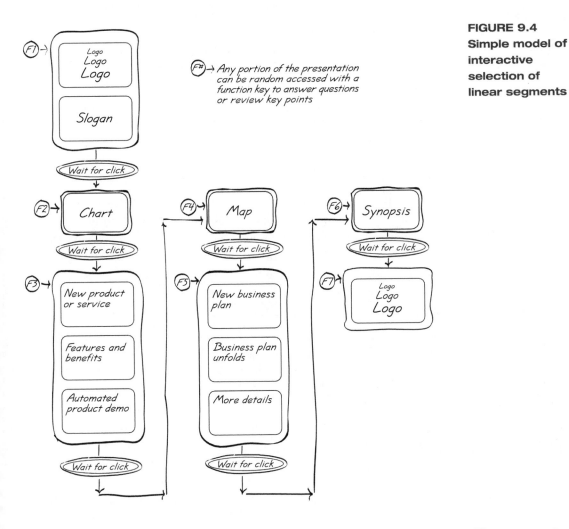

FIGURE 9.4
Simple model of interactive selection of linear segments

Interactivity has the added benefit of structuring information on a want-to-know basis. While a relatively unknown company might present corporate background material in the opening segment, for instance, a well-known organization might tie it to a button on the main screen for those who are curious. This becomes the equivalent of a sidebar in a magazine article. Only those people interested in viewing that angle access it, freeing the main information track to focus efficiently on the nucleus of the message.

Viewers can navigate to specialized segments

Balance the number of levels and items on a screen

Interface design should be simple and intuitive, leaving no question in the user's mind as to functionality. Research has shown that the number of choices on any given screen should be restricted to *nine* options—fewer if possible. Numerous options are best accommodated through nested hierarchical levels. Conversely, too many levels can frustrate and lose viewers, so a balance must be struck. Ideally, users should be made more comfortable by providing some reference as to where they are in the production.

Employ intuition and continuity

As with linear production, the screens shown in various paths should exhibit design continuity. Navigation aids such as buttons should also have similar appearance and position on every screen in which they appear. It is good design practice to provide the user with pause options during linear passages and an exit button throughout. The user should also be given positive reinforcement that a button has been selected through the use of a subtle sound or alternate button graphic.

Use the medium to its fullest potential

Finally, evaluate if the medium is being used to the fullest extent. Since people don't like to read as much in this age of television, for example, consider presenting detailed information in the form of narration or video rather than text (where feasible). (See Figure 9.5.) Similarly, the interactive interface design should play as much as possible on the human fondness for exploration.

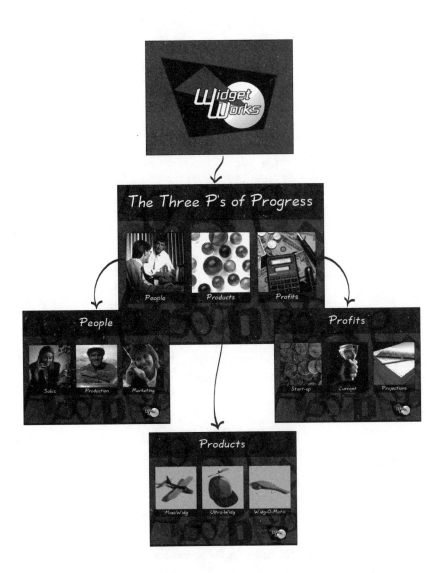

FIGURE 9.5
Example of
nested levels
with design
continuity

Mapping an interactive presentation takes a different form than linear
scripting. A method of visualizing the navigation and hierarchical flow
options is required. Idea processing software designed for brainstorming
business ideas can be used for this purpose. Some authoring software itself
uses hierarchical arrangements of icons, allowing you to start with a map
and then flesh it out. You can also do it the old-fashioned way, using a
large white board or index cards pinned to a cork board—an approach
that provides easy access and visualization for the whole production team.

Map interactive flow

Creating a Timeline

Timelines help set realistic goals

Regardless of whether the production is linear or interactive, the other aspect of planning that benefits from visualization is the timeline. The more critical the drop-dead date for the final project, the more critical the timeline. This should be much more detailed than the preliminary version used in the conceptual stage. Dated milestones need to be included for as many elements and tasks as possible. This serves the valuable function of sorting out tasks that are predicated on the prior completion of others, and helps everyone involved see the big picture and the importance of meeting deadlines.

Determining Resources

Add people, equipment, and budget to the timeline

Planning equipment and human resources is integral to mapping out content, timelines, and budgets. On a formidable project, a team should be assembled based on the aesthetic and technical needs of that particular production. Shorter timelines often require a larger team. Equipment purchase or rental needs should be evaluated simultaneously. Team members are often chosen because of their combination of skills and equipment.

Production

Media are are created during production

Production is typically the stage of the project where the pieces of the puzzle are created. In many ways, this part of the process is straightforward, nose-to-the-grindstone stuff if the preproduction planning was done properly.

Establishing Procedures

Establish common nomenclature

Several procedures should be established at the beginning of production and carried throughout the process. One is to establish standards for file names and where they are stored. A file name that is recognizable when created may seem completely elusive later or when someone else has to find it. The same thing goes for disk labels. Creating a similar storage system for folders, subdirectories, or separate media also helps keep things organized.

It is usually advisable to have team members create media elements in high resolution, even if lower-resolution versions will be used in the actual production. While this can take more time, storage, and processing power, it's much better to have the highest quality source files if portions of the production ever need to be repurposed. Similarly, saving versions on completion of each step in the process makes it easier to make modifications, create a family of similar elements, or recover from mistakes (speaking of which, regular backups are just as important in multimedia production as any other type of computer work).

Create quality source files with the future in mind

Think Ahead and Test Theories

What often appears to be leading-edge technology has a habit of proving to be bleeding edge instead. The technology is changing so rapidly that working with new tools seems to be a way of life. Compatibility is occasionally an issue, as seen in these real-world horrors related by producers. In one case, hundreds of graphics files were saved in a file format the authoring package couldn't import. In another, the media-integration package worked with product B and product C as claimed, but not simultaneously.

Test software compatibility

Performance issues are another common source of problems. A certain software package may perform to spec until given the test of real-world production. One producer I know discovered his authoring package was limited to file sizes one-fifth of that required to integrate the entire production. In another, a snazzy new media integration tool bogged to unacceptable speed and frame rates after all the media elements were brought in for simultaneous playback. In one of my projects, I created a complex 3-D scene for a 100-frame sequence only to find that the software du jour took 24 hours to render the first frame. And a client created an entire presentation that looked great on-screen, but the software couldn't print acceptable hard copy for audience handouts.

Test performance and capacity

In all of these unfortunate cases, the discoveries were made well into the project. "Workarounds" were found, but at the expense of stress, budget overages, and lost sleep. The moral is to plan ahead and conduct tests before committing to a path. Create short segments in key areas of the production, then apply the winning formula to the rest. It seems that I start every production by saying to team members "this is the theory. Test

Tests theories before doing lots of work

it and let me see the results." If we're to be sent back to the drawing board, better sooner than later!

Legal Issues

Copyright law addresses legal issues

The legal issues surrounding multimedia are almost identical to those of other media. While the details might fill an entire book on their own, much of it comes down to common sense and courtesy in light of the United States Copyright Act. In the event of any gray areas, it is highly advisable to check with a lawyer versed in copyright law.

Clip and stock media come with licensing agreements

Material that might potentially be used in a production falls into several basic categories. Clip media created specifically for use in multimedia is sold with the license to use the media under certain circumstances, such as any nonbroadcast purpose in which the property is embodied in other property that gives it added value. Each library provider is different, so a review of the terms is prudent. Similarly, stock houses price the temporary licensing of photos, film, and music for each client based on the specifically contracted-for usage only.

Public domain content can be used freely

Media in the public domain is defined as that for which the copyright has expired—typically 50 years after the death of the holder. Media created by the U.S. Government is also in the public domain. Public domain materials can be used without licensing fees, although the process of actually locating and acquiring the material can bear a charge.

Rights to use other content must be negotiated

Any material not created by your team and not falling into any of the above categories should be presumed to be copyrighted property of others. The rights to incorporate these elements into a production must therefore be negotiated. In addition to music, video, film, photos, and other media elements, characters are also typically copyrighted. Using Bugs Bunny as a spokesperson, for example, is a bad idea without first getting permission in writing from Warner Brothers.

Content alteration falls in a gray area

The digital age has spawned many questions over the use of copyrighted material that has been altered. Various legal cases are still determining precedent on this issue. The basic underlying criteria is typically whether the altered version can be recognized as being derived from the original.

Similarly, the legality of incorporating copyrighted material in a larger original work is often determined by the percentage of value.

Copyrighting an original production typically isn't necessary unless the product is for mass distribution. Even in the absence of a copyright, proof of first usage is often enough. In the case of valued intellectual property, it is highly advisable to establish a copyright to eliminate any doubt.

Copyright your work if it is important

Post-production

Post-production is the final phase where the produced elements are assembled into the end product. In traditional video production, for example, it is the phase where the footage and soundtrack are edited together and the special effects are added. In publishing, it is the stage where the final pages are technically prepared for final output. Both cases represent a process sequential to production of the elements. In the desktop multimedia revolution, production and post-production parallel as often as not.

Elements can be integrated after the production phase

Timing is one major focus of post-production. In simple productions, it may just be a matter of ensuring that each segment is displayed for the appropriate amount of time and that the pacing is satisfactory. More complex projects, in which music, narration, and/or sound effects are synchronized with visual elements, require much more fine tuning. Synchronizing the points at which multiple elements start, stop, and coincide in a highly dynamic presentation can be tedious—and often next to impossible without time-based software. If a production using dynamic media is not to be distributed, it is highly advisable to do the post-production work on the exact computer on which the production will be delivered.

Post-production addresses issues of timing

Transitions are also established during post-production. Visual transitions are easy to use improperly given the myriad choices in many software packages. It is best to choose a simple style and adhere to it for continuity. Audio fades are often necessary at segment transitions as well. Soundtrack volumes may also need to be adjusted to be softer during narrative. In interactive projects, audio-visual transitions should ideally be crafted so that passage is smooth as the user navigates from segment to segment.

Transitions are part of post-production

(This ability to randomly invoke fades and transitions according to user actions is supported by only a handful of media-integration packages.)

Performance and memory issues must be addressed

The complexity of ensuring smooth audio-visual performance on the computer often requires planning ahead. RAM limitations often require that large productions be loaded in segments. The associated delays, however, can cause distraction in interactive projects and disrupt the flow of linear productions. Many media integration packages support preloading of specified media elements or segments. In linear productions, the trick is to find or create natural pauses in the content flow that provide the opportunity to preload files in the background. With interactivity, preloading can even involve loading the next portion of all possible branches the user may choose.

Testing

Testing of technical performance is essential

The final phase in post-production is testing. If the production is to be played back on a computer other than the development machine, it should be tested on the target machine or any known variations of configuration. If the production is to be mass distributed, even more extensive testing is required. In interactive projects, all possible branches should be tested to ensure that buttons and segments have been linked properly.

Productions should always be tested with audiences

Testing should also be conducted on the effectiveness of the production. If a marketing message is being presented, a trial run with objective parties can provide valuable feedback. Productions that are to be mass distributed require mass testing to ensure that the user interface is properly intuited by the audience and the expected results are returned. Similarly, interactive training projects require testing for comprehension and verification of scoring.

10

Business Presentations

Presentations are currently the single largest application for multimedia in business. That's because companies always have a message to communicate, whether it's to staff, stockholders, trading partners, distributors, the media, or consumers. Given the rapid pace of today's business world and increasingly powerful presentation software, business presentations are the most likely form of multimedia that managers and other business professionals will actually create themselves.

Presentations drive the business multimedia market

Presentation Power

Slide shows and overhead transparencies are time-honored staples in presenting business messages. There are several major compelling reasons for making the leap to computer-controlled presentations—malleability, cost-saving, and impact.

Computer-based presentations offer major benefits

Malleability

Business communicators today must be light on their feet. Let's face it— the world can change every time you pick up the phone! Moreover, facts and statistics can change right up to the last minute. Electronic presentation technology allows changes to be made right up to presentation time. A traveling sales presentation can have a placeholder into which the current prospect or company name can be entered before each pitch. Charts linked directly to spreadsheets are automatically regenerated when new data is entered to reflect late-breaking figures. By extension, an executive on the road could download new spreadsheet statistics from the main office before a meeting and have the charts automatically reflect the current figures. Slides can be re-sorted with a few mouse clicks rather than by emptying a slide carrousel and starting over. It is even possible to create a presentation from scratch on an airplane using a laptop, and you deliver the presentation on arrival! In short, multimedia presentations facilitate "just-in-time" marketing.

Computer-based presentations yield tremendous flexibility

In addition to polishing a presentation for one-time delivery, presentation software also easily facilitates reshaping a presentation for different audiences. While the information presented to stockholders, employees, and customers may contain different components, it is likely that many of the needed elements will be the same. Electronic media in general provide cut-and-paste, mix-and-match flexibility. Presentations created specifically with modularity in mind can further amortize the investment of time and money in elements such as flying logos, animated graphics, video clips, and so forth. As another example, a simple change of master template can globally alter the overall background, font, or color scheme to suit different audiences according to gender, age, or ethnic background while retaining the same message. Today's global business environment and domestic ethnic-niche marketing also means that translated text can be dropped into an otherwise stock presentation.

Cost

*Computer-based
presentations can be
less expensive than
slides*

Before the proliferation of desktop computers, outside production companies charged thousands of dollars to create and output slide presentations. Over the past decade, software packages like Aldus Persuasion, Microsoft Powerpoint, and SPC's Harvard Graphics have allowed business people to use the computers on their desks to transform standard outlines into files that service bureaus can turn into a series of slides or overheads. The average cost is $6 to $10 per slide for normal turnaround, and each "build" that adds a new point to the same image requires a separate slide. Last minute changes or additions incur additional rush charges—up until the point there's simply no time left to implement changes. All totaled, a complete show can run hundreds and even thousands of dollars in output charges. (The purchase of an in-house film recorder can range from $6,000 to $20,000 and requires an operator.) These same programs can be used to deliver the presentation directly from the computer—obviating the cost and logistics of slide output altogether.

Use existing elements

Looking at the big picture, many businesses supplement printed communication with other media such as video, television, and radio. Investment in creating content for these media can be amortized by including dynamic elements in a multimedia presentation.

Impact

The phrase "image is everything" most certainly applies to presentations. Presentations in general lend a larger-than-life air to the presenter. The most rudimentary image improvement that computer-based presentations offer over slides is the fact that monitors and most late-model LCD projectors don't require the near darkness that can disorient viewers. Many setups can employ both computer graphics and video sources using a single screen. Moreover, laptops with color LCD displays allow you to make a presentation virtually anywhere.

There are physical advantages over slides and tape decks

Any one of the plethora of transitions available in presentation packages is a vast improvement over the pop to black and accompanying "kachunk" sound associated with slide projectors. Animation and digital video help illustrate concepts and immediately set the presentation apart from the standard bill of fare. Charts can grow over time. Motion paths allow elements like text and images to fly into place. While soundtracks can accompany slide presentations, direct support for audio files can help ensure synchronization and simplicity. Interactivity makes it easy to locate specific points for review—and you can even structure presentations with an interactive interface and hierarchy that break the monotonous slide-show mold completely and engages the viewer.

Dynamic media and interactivity greatly improve audience interest

Delivery Strategies

While there are many universal delivery issues, the categories of staged meetings, field delivery, and remote delivery merit special consideration.

Staged Meetings

Since presentations are no longer restricted to traditional slide shows, there are many possibilities for delivery. The most common, however, is still the typical meeting ranging in size from boardroom to ballroom—usually delivered with live narrative. It is highly advisable to use the same computer to deliver the presentation as the one on which it was developed (or tested), since variations such as installed fonts, RAM, CPU speeds, display adapters, and sound cards can cause unexpected problems. Alternately, at least try to bring a portable hard drive or removable media drive with your operating system, software, and utilities as well as the

Use known and tested equipment when possible

presentation. Regardless of hardware, the more important the presentation, the more setup time you should plan on!

Choose the projection system as well

A standard computer monitor is only effective with an audience of several people. Larger monitors in the 25" to 40" range offer excellent fidelity for medium-sized audiences, but are rare and hard to transport. For larger audiences, it is advisable to supply the projection system or rent one with specific capabilities. Staged meetings often utilize a pair of converged rear-screen projectors, but require professional alignment when moved. Transparent LCD panels designed to fit on overhead projectors are the most popular for more impromptu presentations. Most of these require a projector with at least 4,000 lumens for the proper brightness, contrast, and color fidelity. By contrast, there are plenty of older low-power overhead projectors lurking around that can reduce the most ambitious production to a mere ghost of itself.

Field Delivery

Laptops allow presentation deliveries almost anywhere

Portable computers provide an easy means for taking presentations on the road. Virtually anywhere can become a presentation environment—a prospect's office, a hotel room, the trade-show floor, or even a taxi cab. Portability also makes it easy to modify the presentation in transit. (Note, however, that the short battery life of laptops is reduced even further by multimedia elements such as digital video that constantly access the hard disk.) One trick that works very nicely in a series of client presentations, for example, is customizing one of the opening screens with the client's personal or company name to make it look like the whole presentation was created just for them.

Dynamic presentations push laptops to their limits

One of the first decisions is the choice of equipment. Lugging desktop computers is a difficult proposition. Simple slide-show style presentations can be played back on just about any laptop, with color capabilities being an obvious preference. By contrast, dynamic presentations push the envelope. You'll want a laptop (or lunchbox-style computer) with an active matrix LCD panel in order to play animation and video smoothly. You'll also want a machine with the fastest processor you can afford, a decent amount of RAM, and a fast hard drive with moderate capacity.

While some laptops have small internal speakers, they lack the power and fidelity required to deliver soundtracks effectively. While larger speakers are desirable, you may wish to compromise on a pair that fits into a travel bag with the computer and any other components. The LCD display will only serve as an adequate viewing device for two or three people, so you'll also need display circuitry that will allow connection to an external monitor—or travel with your own LCD projection panel and projector.

Include speakers and display options in your hardware roundup

Remote Delivery

In a world of overnight mail and immediate faxes, it's no surprise that presentations are being delivered remotely. Most presentation packages include a run-time player that can be distributed freely with your presentation, so the viewer doesn't have to own the software you've used. Presentation packages supporting digitized sound are particularly suited for the job, since they allow prerecorded narration to be delivered in lieu of a live spokesperson.

Run-time players facilitate remote delivery of presentations

The greatest challenge in remote delivery is equipment and configuration compatibility. The choice of delivery medium becomes the first challenge. As discussed in Chapter 3, the lowest common denominator of the floppy disk severely restricts the size and quality of the content. The rapid growth of the CD-ROM installed base—as well as the plummeting price of CD-ROM recorders—makes it increasingly more feasible to deliver via this medium. Here, again, there are performance variables such as single- or double-speed CD-ROM players that may affect the performance of dynamic media. The safest bet is instructing viewers to copy files to their hard drive for playback.

Delivery medium presents the greatest challenge

Overall variables in CPU and other system performance areas often warrant a conservative approach to included media, or the use of scalable technologies such as QuickTime or AVI. The aforementioned use of sound implies that the viewer's machine has audio playback capability. Incorporation of digital video requires system-level support for video playback and a machine with enough power to deliver decent video. Proper text display also requires that the appropriate fonts be installed. The safest approach is to include these system-level elements on the delivery medium with specific instructions on their installation—better yet, include an executable file that performs the installation.

Consider additional variables

11

Major Productions

Trade-Show Productions

Anyone who has ever exhibited at a trade show knows that it's a high-stakes proposition. The expense of the floor space, booth design and construction, and travel budgets for participants can be formidable. Not only is it important to make an impact, but the exhibit must compete with others for the attention of the attendees. Many companies have found that employing AV technology has helped create a competitive edge, but multimedia tools can up the ante in attracting and holding a crowd.

Multimedia ups the ante on standard use of audio and video at trade shows

Staged Productions

The current paradigm in attracting attention for most trade-show booths of any size is the combination of one or more live actors with one or more large video screens. (The use of live actors over canned narration adds a human touch, another level of depth, a forum for audience interaction, and a vehicle for the ever-popular merchandise giveaways.) On the top end of the scale, companies with large booths sometimes create a theater environment where a very large screen is used to deliver a production more resembling a movie—often without the use of actors. The secret here is the anticipation of waiting in line for a show combined with a captive audience in an enclosed and darkened theater. And on smaller scales, computer-based productions are often used as attractor loops to draw people in, present some of the message, and generate enough interest to speak with booth personnel.

Multimedia often supplements or replaces video at trade shows

Video replaced slides as the standard visual medium; however, the use of computers for multimedia delivery on the screens has several additional advantages. The first benefit is that computer-based productions are more flexible up to the last minute, since video production for the trade-show level typically requires a full studio. (Note that the more reliant a production is on audio-visual synchronization, the more difficult it is to modify under pressure.) I've done computer-based productions where a client VP signed off on the work, only to have the CEO request a modification the

Computer-based productions are more flexible than video

night before the show opening—3,000 miles away from where the majority of the work was done.

Interactivity provides more flexibility during delivery

Interactivity is an equally compelling reason for computer-based delivery. Given today's tools, the lines between presentations and more ambitious productions are becoming increasingly blurred. Simple pause-and-advance style interaction can be useful in productions in which bullet points are displayed and discussed or audience participation is encouraged. A high-tech effect can be gleaned through the use of interactive screens that the actor uses to navigate to linear dynamic production segments.

Interactivity also increases audience interest

The ultimate in interactivity is getting the audience directly involved. Audience response systems that provide keypads for each seat can be used to collect responses to queries, then display the collated responses on a screen. Since these products are primarily designed as stand-alone systems, it's typically easier to use a separate computer and display system for the polling and results rather than trying to integrate the data into the main production. Another use for interactivity at trade shows is in staging game shows having to do with the product or service being presented. Computers can be used to display the quiz or puzzle material, poll the players, and display answers and scores.

Computer-based productions can be more cost effective than video

Cost-effective production also drives the use of multimedia at shows. Even in linear productions, computer-based tools can often turn out a production that is more compelling than traditional video for a given budget. That's because decent-quality video can cost a lot to stage, edit, and produce regardless of how it's displayed. Moreover, the plethora of special effects to which audiences have become accustomed in television and film has raised expectations above pedestrian video productions. In creative hands, computer-based tools can be used to generate graphics, photo montages, animations, soundtracks, and digital video effects that tell the story a different way for potentially less money.

Finally, computers can be used to automate the various elements of major productions. Computers are capable of controlling lighting, video transports, audio levels, monitor switching, and even hydraulics and motors in staged shows. While this level of complexity usually requires a professional staging team and multiple computers, this application can ensure smooth, repeatable performances and create results that would require much more labor to do manually.

Computers can control the entire staging of advanced productions

There are several caveats about using computers to deliver trade show productions. First, the audience doesn't care about the technology behind the curtain—only the viewing experience. Smooth animation, synchronization, and full-fidelity digital audio and video require formidable computing power and audio-visual hardware. In productions sophisticated enough for large audiences, it is strongly advisable to use the exact computer for which the production has been optimized. Second, computers are still more volatile than video decks and a glitch or crash is bad news with an audience watching. Finally, don't let the promise of desktop technology overshadow the creativity of the message. The sophistication of most trade shows requires contracting a professional producer to guarantee the best results and return on investment.

There are still drawbacks to using computers for major productions

Kiosks

The foregoing discussion properly implies that audience participation is the most effective method of getting the message across. Many companies are using interactive multimedia kiosks at trade shows to attract attention and encourage interaction. This has a cumulative effect as people walking by see others doing something interesting and are drawn in by sheer curiousity. While computers alone can be used for this task, encasing them in a decorative housing adds much more uniqueness and mystique.

Kiosks invite audience involvement

Kiosks typically present an *attractor loop*, which calls attention to itself and invites a bystander to request more information. Once someone responds via touchscreen, mouse, or other input device, the viewer is usually presented with navigation options matching areas of interest. The viewer

Kiosks use attractor loops, navigation, and time outs

selects the desired path and the computer presents a brief track—enough to get the point across and generate interest, yet not enough to risk boredom. Good interface design dictates that users be given a method to cancel out of a segment and navigate elsewhere on demand. In parallel, all navigation screens should time out after a modest time interval of no interaction and restart the attractor in assumption that the viewer has left.

The attractor loop should attract attention

Content design for kiosks depends upon the nature of the situation. The attractor loop should typically have a high dynamic level through the use of moving imagery and up-tempo music. Short productions using the music video style are good hooks, for example. Few attractor loops need be longer than one minute before restarting automatically. The human appeal of narration inviting interaction is usually more successful than graphics and text alone. (Installation location is important to consider, however: loops with audio content can irritate employees in tight quarters to the point where they'll do something as rash as pulling the plug!)

Kiosks can provide selective information for different viewers

Here's an example of a typical trade-show kiosk. The attractor loop draws attention and attracts a viewer. Responding to the invitation, the viewer touches the touchscreen to signal his presence and is then presented with navigation options such as several product lines, company background, and ordering information. Touching one of the product line buttons navigates to a submenu containing buttons for each product. Alternately, touching the company background button summons a linear segment touting the wonders of the organization. Finally, touching the ordering info button could display a map in which you touch your home state to summon a list of stores or an introduction to the area rep (see Figure 11.1).

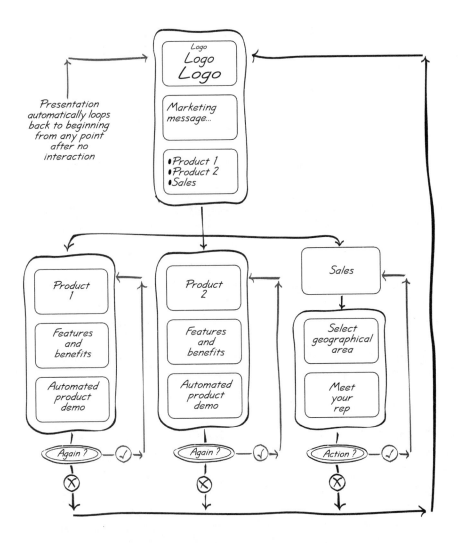

FIGURE 11.1
Example of
interactive kiosk
flow

Presentation
automatically loops
back to beginning
from any point
after no
interaction

Aside from merely presenting information, the computer provides an excellent means for gathering data as well. On the simple end, market testing can be accommodated by tracking how much time was spent in each navigation branch over the course of the show and collating the results. On the next level, additional questions can be posed with yes/no or multiple choice answers for statistical collation. Free-form user entry is the most difficult to accommodate, partially from a programming standpoint and partially because it requires an entry vehicle in the form of a standard QWERTY keyboard or an on-screen representation that is activiated with a mouse, trackball, or touchscreen. When programmed

Kiosks can also be used to acquire information

properly, however, this implementation can provide feedback such as name, address, phone, profile, and purchase plans. Networked kiosks open the possibility for multiple users to interact with one another—one possible permutation being multi-player games based on the marketing message.

Computers as Video Production Tools

Video is more reliable than computers for final delivery

There's no rule that says multimedia has to be interactive, or that the results can't be delivered on videotape. Dumping productions created completely within the computer onto tape has the advantage of increased stability. In the case of a power anomaly, for example, a video deck might simply glitch or someone might have to hit the Play button again in the worst case. Computers are typically less tolerant and tend to crash under similar circumstances—forcing a reboot, entailing program reload and (typically) playback from the beginning of the production. And if Murphy had lived in the Information Age his law of computing would imply that a computer will run perfectly until the point where unattributable glitches will cause the greatest embarrassment. Moreover, it's easier for the average person to spec video gear for rental and play tapes than deal with computers.

Linear videotape is still the most common delivery medium

The look at video tools in Chapter 3 also reveals that digital video editing and multimedia production packages can make video production more cost-effective by bringing much of the work in-house. Linear videotape is still the lowest common denominator in delivering messages remotely to people. A production primarily designed for trade-show delivery, for example, is often repurposed for distribution to key clients or prospects. Multimedia production tools allow relatively easy edits and modifications before creating video for the masses.

12

Training

Benefits of Computer-Based Training

Realization by large corporations that audio-visual training saves time and money was one of the driving forces behind the rise of industrial video, as well as the CBT (computer-based training) industry. The basic benefits are twofold and apply to multimedia as well. First, the money otherwise spent on endless repetition of classes by live instructors could be spent once in creating a far superior product on video. This is especially beneficial and cost-effective in situations such as fast-food chains where employee turnover is high and the locations are remote. Second, video can offer significantly better visualization and overall presentation aesthetics, fostering greater retention. (There are a growing number of service bureaus specializing in converting existing training videos to interactive CD-ROM for improved personal delivery and archiving.)

Training via audio-visual saves money and is better retained

The advantages of integrating multimedia computing into training environments have several benefits over video alone. The oldest incarnation of multimedia in training was the use of text-based computers to control laserdisc players in presenting a passage on a dedicated video monitor, then testing via text queries on the computer monitor. Digital video technology makes it possible to display everything within a single computer monitor, and with greater synergy, aesthetics, and impact.

Multimedia makes audio-visual training self-contained

The most compelling case is the ability to automatically test for comprehension and offer remedial lessons on the fly. Today's training software also permits the authoring of courseware sophisticated enough to test comprehension after each lesson, display appropriate remedial segments on failures, log placeholders to which each student can return in extensive courses, and grade and print final scores on course completion. Material can also be edited with greater ease than with video, and lesson modules can easily be combined as required for the learning needs of different people and departments.

CBT permits more effective learning paradigms

Internal Training

Electronic training suits situations where one message reaches many people

In general, a good case for multimedia training can be made in any scenario where a reasonable number of people need access to similar information that is best presented in audio-visual form. The specific applications for in-house training are as diverse as the number of different industries and businesses. Perhaps the most common application is training on equipment operation and manufacturing processes such as those found in factory assembly lines. Government mandates regarding things like recycling, workstation ergonomics, food handling, and safe handling of toxic materials make automated training a logical solution. Many companies are electronically implementing more generic information such as corporate style guides and employee handbooks, combining search operations with audio-visual presentation of the requested information (see Figure 12.1). More altruistic training content includes subjects such as interpersonal communication skills, stress management, and personal growth—often in the form of interactive role playing and games.

Chains use CBT to ensure uniformity with high-employee turnover

High-profile companies with multiple retail locations such as fast-food and retail chains are particularly sensitive to the needs of training since they must exercise control over a high-turnover network of relatively unskilled labor. A food chain, for example, might implement training on health regulations and preparation of proprietary dishes. A retail chain might train on customer courtesy, store policies, product knowledge, and salesmanship.

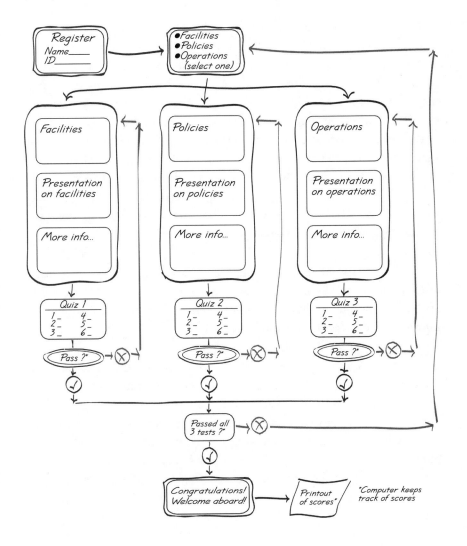

FIGURE 12.1
Simple example
of CBT design

FIGURE 12.1
Simple example
of CBT design

Register
Name____
ID_____

● Facilities
● Policies
● Operations
(select one)

Facilities

Presentation
on facilities

More info...

Policies

Presentation
on policies

More info...

Operations

Presentation
on operations

More info...

Quiz 1
1__ 4__
2__ 5__
3__ 6__

Quiz 2
1__ 4__
2__ 5__
3__ 6__

Quiz 3
1__ 4__
2__ 5__
3__ 6__

Pass ?*

Pass ?*

Pass ?*

Passed all
3 tests ?*

Congratulations!
Welcome aboard!

Printout
of scores*

*Computer keeps
track of scores

Training can take place on the desktop

In-house training can take several forms. Dedicated training centers are still viable, with networking making it possible for instructors to monitor students' progress from a master station. Given the proliferation of multimedia computing on more and more desktops, however, many training materials can be viewed in a corporate employee's normal workspace via CD-ROM when needed in the course of everyday work. This contrasts to the need for dedicated equipment such as VCRs and laserdisc players in more traditional scenarios. Improved multimedia server technologies and CD-ROM jukeboxes are also beginning to make it feasible to access training materials via LANs. Remote training for retail stores is currently best facilitated via CD-ROM at a dedicated training station, with updates taking the form of updated CD-ROM mailings.

Portable players facilitate field training

Field training is another growing application for multimedia, largely due to technology such as laptops and self-contained portable CD-ROM players. Service businesses, in particular, can benefit from just-in-time information on recent models or methods.

The information superhighway makes distance learning feasible

By extension, companies with national and international sites have found it useful to implement distance learning—a video transmission from a central location to classrooms at multiple offices. To date, only an elite group of corporations has been implementing distance learning since it has only been feasible via expensive satellite transmissions and leased phone lines. As the information superhighway takes shape, it will lower the bar for distance learning since the requirements will be largely fulfilled by soon-to-be everyday communications technology. This will probably also become the vehicle for retail training, as well.

Outside Training

Multimedia facilitates training of new retail staff

Product manufacturers are in constant need of effective methods of training people who are not under their direct employ. Manufacturers have traditionally spent a great deal of money on training retail salespeople on products and services via in-person calls, factory seminars, and, more recently, videotape. The rapid turnover of salespeople in retail makes automated training more sensible since the material can be viewed by new personnel on a schedule dictated by store management.

This training vehicle also makes tremendous sense for manufacturers who have a large and rapidly changing product line. Consumer electronics stores are prime examples. While there are certainly some salespeople who really know their products, the number of models by various manufacturers can be overwhelming. Manufacturers who provide training in general stand a much greater chance of engendering themselves to retailers. Those who take the extra step of having that information random-accessible for reference during a sale further up the ante.

Manufacturers with changing product lines increase sales through training

Electronic training also becomes viable when large volumes of service data are involved. I recently received a call from a large auto manufacturer querying the feasibility of putting service instructions for several decades' worth of their car models on CD-ROM for their franchisees. The service recommendations and installation procedures for the sheer number of parts involved was enough to warrant moving away from paper merely from the standpoint of cost, size, and shipping weight. The added benefits of easy updates, fast searches, and visualization of complex installation procedures was perceived as an excellent bonus.

Service industries benefit from random access to vast amounts of data

The "how-to" training concept is also being applied to other types of service providers. Another call I received recently was from a company that nationally franchises a rug and drapery cleaning business. They wanted videos of specific solutions to cleaning problems (such as red wine spots on white carpet) to be available on demand via laptops for their franchisees to use on-site. Similarly, I know of building contractors who are interested in having documentaries of specialized construction and repair tasks available on-site via laptops. The list goes on, extending to virtually any situation where instant access and visualization can justify the cost.

Many industries can benefit from instruction on-site and on demand

The big issue with noncompany sites is playback equipment and budgets. Stores will rarely see training in one manufacturer's product as a large enough benefit to pay for dedicated hardware. Manufacturers can raise the incentive by including valuable generic training in topics such as prospecting, qualifying, and closing. Similarly, few manufacturers are interested in the expenditure necessary to provide equipment dedicated to training alone across many locations. One solution is to ammortize the investment in a kiosk that can also serve as a consumer point-of-sale device as described later in this chapter. On tight budgets, the sensible thing to do

Getting playback equipment into noncompany locations requires creativity

is produce for a standard medium such as an MPC system, which the retailer owns or can be convinced to upgrade for training as well as business. (With field service industries, a multimedia laptop is appropriate.) Set-top boxes are viable in some cases where motion is not required (Kodak Photo CD) or where the mastering cost can be ammortized across many installations (Philips CD-I, 3DO, and so on) with MPEG.

Linear videotape is a worst-case option

If all else fails, multimedia tools can be used to produce linear videotapes that can be mass-produced and distributed to salespeople on VHS for store or home viewing. An alternative in the case of service industries is producing 8mm or Hi-8 for use with hand-held players or camcorders sporting color LCD panels.

13

Reaching the Consumer

While information within and between businesses is currently the largest industrial market for multimedia applications, the technology is taking a natural evolution to reaching the mass-consumer market. This momentum is taking two logical forms—electronic retailing and direct marketing. Either can use the technology passively or interactively.

Multimedia is used in retailing and direct marketing

Retail Applications

Multimedia in retail can be categorized as passive or interactive information, or interactive vending of goods.

Passive Uses

Signage is a staple of retailing, covering everything from glamorizing to special pricing. In the 1980s, the advent of the music video genre and inexpensive VCRs took the next step by lending a dance club effect to clothing stores and departments while promoting fashion. Video players and monitors also popped up in retail situations ranging from hardware stores to grocery produce departments to hawk products overtly or more subtly by illustrating techniques using the products. LCD strips with moving banners were another sign of the times. Multimedia technology can be seen and used passively as an extension of this trend in one-to-many communication (see Figure 13.1).

Passive multimedia used in retailing can reach many people

**FIGURE 13.1
Example of linear
loop for
electronic
signage**

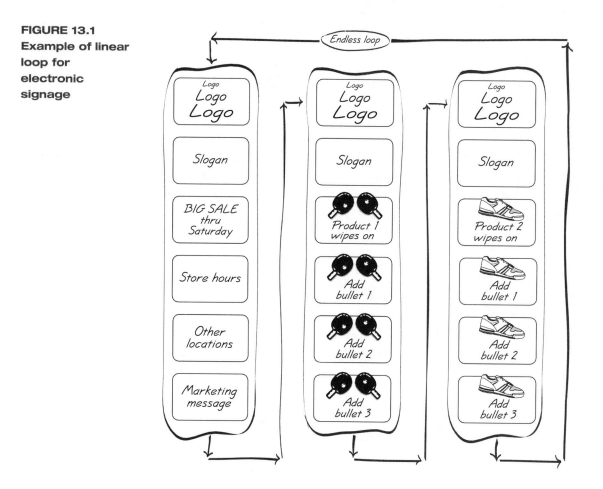

*Multimedia can
instantly customize
ads*

The advantage of multimedia over video is that it can be interactive to the retailer while appearing passive to customers. While videotapes are cast in stone, a retailer can employ multimedia technology to program a series of signs and ads on demand with relative ease from preproduced elements stored on disk. This customizing can work at the level of a given week, special promotion, or even to help close a specific customer. The program could also be structured to implement simple signage announcing instant sales and new merchandise. By extension, modem technology can currently be used to effect global changes in the displays of all stores in a chain or region thereof!

Several technology advances will add power and momentum to this use of multimedia. Large format flat screens will likely begin replacing CRTs in the next few years, with their shallow profile making for easier placement in stores. The information superhighway should also make it feasible for narrowcasts (programming aimed at a small subset of the population) created in production facilities to be sent directly to remote locations in real time.

Flat panel displays will further aid electronic retailing

Grocery stores once test marketed the effectiveness of video monitors in check-out lines. The effect was more one of promotion than of immediate sales since nobody in line is anxious to lose their place to go get something else. While the best way to reach the consumer was in the aisles, shelf space is at a premium. The solution? Some grocery chains are now testing LCD panels mounted directly on the carts that display unique ads narrowcast for each aisle or section using wireless technology. While the current technology employs slow, passive monochrome LCD panels (due to cost), the proliferation of active color LCD panels will someday make it possible for full-blown TV-style ads to come to a grocery cart near you.

Wireless technology and LCD panels can yield personalized ads

Interactive Uses

The incorporation of interactivity brings the true power of multimedia to retailing. In the 1980s, car manufacturers were one of the first industries to use the fledgling technology in the form of laserdisc players showing promotional videos for specific models on demand. Today's multimedia technology streamlines this type of application by incorporating navigation and information on a single screen in a kiosk. The hardware is typically housed in an attractive kiosk so that customers and salespeople alike need "pay no attention to the man behind the curtain." The use of touchscreens allows users to simply touch an on-screen item for more information, thereby eliminating any interface issues and fear of technology (see Figure 13.2). Add the storage capacity of hard disks and CD-ROM and you have an information source that customers can interact with themselves when no salespeople are available.

Kiosks can help close sales

**FIGURE 13.2
Simple example
of retail kiosk
flow**

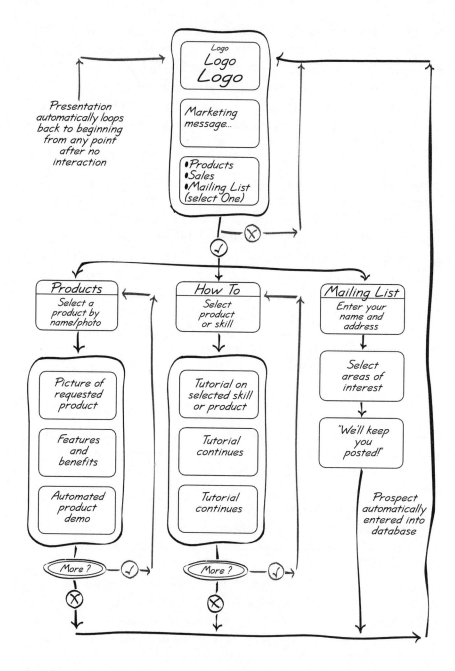

*Computers can
display product
information*

Another benefit of kiosks is that they can act as an aid for salespeople. How, for example, are you supposed to choose between 40 models of VCR when you walk into a consumer electronics store? The salespeople usually don't have comprehensive knowledge of all the product lines and literature is often not available. In this situation, kiosks would allow customers to navigate to the product category and locate information that would help zero in on the best model for their needs. A simple kiosk would provide menu items for each model and produce a virtual brochure for the selected item.

One of the mandates of new technology is to use it to its greatest effectiveness over other media. The aforementioned virtual brochure could take the form of an audio-visual ad, and even be made interactive so that customers can still easily query specific features. More ambitious use of the technology would be to present an overview of feature sets across various models, setting the stage for the customer to understand options categorically and the benefits of various functions for certain applications. The customer could respond that specific features are important for their application, a search would automatically be conducted for products matching the desired feature set, and information about the qualifying product(s) would be presented.

Kiosks can interactively target the right product for the customer

Stores such as department stores often carry more merchandise than can currently be displayed or stocked. Kiosks sporting electronic catalogs provide an efficient means of storing and accessing all of the permutations. Moreover, audio-visual sales pitches can take the place of mundane print. Some department stores have also used rather pedestrian computer technology to keep track of bridal registries. The process of choosing the right gift could be greatly enhanced through the addition of multimedia elements that aid in visualization.

Multimedia can display electronic catalogs

To stores selling computers, coming up with the hardware to run automated sales aids isn't a problem. For other retailers, much of the key to justifying the expenditure for multimedia technology and production is to ammortize the investment across several purposes. Almost all good kiosk designs incorporate an attractor loop that automatically kicks in when no one is using the station. This not only serves to attract attention and draw people in, but can also be used as an advertising medium—for house ads or even those paid for and provided by suppliers. Similarly, kiosks can do double duty as tools for sales training in off hours or for electronic signage as described earlier in this chapter. They can also incorporate directories in the case of large venues such as malls, department stores, and resorts, which helps to eliminate customer inconvenience and staff distractions.

Investments in kiosk technology can be ammortized to other uses

Kiosks can also be used to acquire customer data	Yet another way to maximize the investment in interactive technology is data acquisition. On an overview level, kiosk content can be designed to track how people move through the system, thereby revealing interest trends. On a much more finite level, the kiosk can ask users to input their contact information. This can be done in tandem to querying specific demographic questions or transparently tracking their interest in certain types of products according to navigation choices. The results can be added to a database, which can then be accessed via LAN or modem for follow-up.
Multimedia technology can also aid "what-if" visualization	Multimedia and related technologies are also being used in other areas of retailing, especially as an aid to visualization. Image processing and 3-D rendering technology is being used in home improvement centers to do make-overs from photographs of a customer's home before the customer buys supplies. On the exterior, landscapes can be replanted on-screen, and siding can be textured and painted. On the interior, new fabric can be mapped onto furniture, lighting can be altered, and wallpaper and new paint colors can be mapped onto walls. Similarly, services are emerging that do computerized make-overs of clients at hair salons and make-up counters. While these technologies currently require store personnel to operate, the same technology can be used for the other multimedia retailing functions discussed here.
Kiosk design must address physical as well as content concerns	Kiosks are essentially locked, custom-designed boxes that house a multimedia-capable computer, touchscreen, storage media, and a sound system if audio is to be used. In addition to content, kiosk designers must consider such things as construction aesthetics, power source, security, ventilation, protection from the elements, and access to a phone line if modems are to be used. Touchscreens are logical choices for interaction, since they solve two problems. First, there are still many people who aren't comfortable with computer input devices such as keyboards and mice. Second, they are more impervious to the abuse that must be expected of anything unattended and exposed to the public.
Kiosk designers must consider content update paths	As for content updates, there are currently several solutions. Hard disks provide the fastest response time, and it's not a bad idea to put often-accessed information and semipermanent, high-throughput segments such as animated attractor loops on these devices. Updates can be deliv-

ered via CD-ROM, either played directly on demand or copied to the hard disk with every update. Updates can be made directly to the hard disk in local situations via removable media or networks, and to remote locations via modem.

The Automated Salesperson

From the use of electronics as marketing tools and sales aids, the next logical step is having a kiosk handle the entire transaction, especially those that are mundane. When it comes down to it, the ubiquitous ATM machine is a node in a network of fairly pedestrian PCs with specialized peripherals. Some are already more oriented to color graphics than others, and it's a short leap to using these machines to play commercials during attractor loops and while transactions are being processed. Similarly, many states having lottery games have kiosks that accept dollar bills and vend lottery tickets in grocery stores and other high-traffic retail stores. While the technology by no means falls on the cutting edge of multimedia in most cases, it's a logical step to include video attractor loops depicting the alleged empowerment of wealth.

Kiosks are already part of our lives as consumers

Kiosks are also proliferating in video rental chains. The initial application is helping customers find the right movie—either by directly requesting to view a promo clip of a specific title or by interactively navigating through preferred genres to view clips of suggested movies. The addition of vending technology makes it possible for the same machine to accept money or plastic and deliver the selected tape. This will become even more viable as movies become available in smaller sizes on CD-ROM. The same logic can be applied to music CDs, software, and video games.

Multimedia can be effective in electronic vending

Desktop technology has helped give rise to the concept of customized products on demand in areas such as publishing, music, video, and presentation. Customization in automated vending is also beginning to appear. One visible example is the Personics kiosk, found in some major music retail chains, that allows users to audition and select a sequence of songs from various artists, which are then compiled into a custom tape while the customer waits. Hallmark has made a commitment to vending machines that allow consumers to select from preset card designs on screen, enter custom names and messages, and print a unique card. Some musical instrument stores now have kiosks that laser print sheet music on

The next step is vending of customized items on demand

demand after auditioning the arrangement—a process that has significant advantages when it comes to stocking. It is probable that this phenomenon will extend into on-demand custom manufacturing in other areas such as art and clothing.

Direct Marketing

Cable TV provides examples of direct marketing programs

Direct marketing is a coveted method of reaching consumers because it cuts out the middleman and gives the product or service providers more control. Once relegated to telephone campaigns, print ads, and costly television spots, direct marketing has taken a major turn with the proliferation of cable TV. Home shopping channels and paid *infomercials* are now entrenched as valued avenues for reaching and selling directly to consumers.

Multimedia computers will proliferate enough to be viable marketing tools

Just as cable represented a new entry into consumers' living rooms, new conduits are emerging that hold the key to using multimedia technology for direct marketing. The installed base of home and business computers with multimedia capabilities and CD-ROM drives is skyrocketing, enough to make direct marketing via mailed CD-ROMs viable. While the installed base for generic computers with floppy drives alone is much higher, multimedia capabilities and CD-ROM capacity are usually required in order to make a computer-based presentation aesthetically compelling. (Companies like Buick and Jeep have launched marketing campaigns on floppy disk that do not rely heavily on sound, video, or photography.)

Modems offer information on demand

Modem connection to on-line services such as CompuServe, America Online, and Prodigy represents another avenue to reach consumers. The proliferation of Internet is also adding momentum to on-line marketing. The plus is that the millions of people browsing these services can access information anytime they want it; the minus is that multimedia data can still currently be prohibitive to download at the speed of the average user's modem. On-line information providers have several workarounds. One is to limit the ambitiousness of their content. The other is to initially download only text and thumbnails for navigation, and then download the requesting information. This problem will gradually dissipate as modems become faster and as the information superhighway ultimately takes shape.

Interactive set-top players offer yet another delivery vehicle for multimedia content in the home. The installed base at this writing, however, is too insignificant to count. Even CD-ROMs and modems cannot yet represent an entire marketing campaign, but instead serve as a piece of the puzzle. A further caveat is that demographic research should first establish that prospects are likely to be receptive to your product or services and have access to a computer. As with modem speed, these issues will gradually fade as interactive technology becomes entrenched in the home.

Electronic marketing is merely a piece of the puzzle

Direct Marketing Applications

One of the major uses for multimedia technology in direct marketing is interactive catalogs. Like their kiosk equivalents, electronic catalogs provide the benefits of easy search capability, product comparisons, audio-visual ads, and more. In general, the multimedia promotional experience has much more life and excitement over print, bearing a greater resemblance to television than to traditional catalogs. Placing catalogs online or on CD-ROM for viewing in consumers' homes is an excellent way to ammortize the investment in in-store catalog kiosks. Electronic delivery also makes tremendous economic sense considering the printing and shipping costs of traditional catalogs. As an added bonus, the information capacity for a given budget is not nearly as finite as with print media.

Multimedia facilitates interactive audio-visual catalogs

The storage capacity of on-line services is so vast that the concept of virtual catalogs can be extended to that of virtual malls containing virtual stores. Two-way communication makes it possible to not only choose the desired product, but complete the transaction by ordering via credit card while on-line. The bandwidth available with the advent of the information superhighway will add tremendous realism, breadth, and depth to the virtual shopping experience.

Two-way communication allows instantaneous purchases

Software manufacturers are currently taking advantage of yet another variation of the virtual store. CD-ROMs are now widely available that contain a variety of commercial software in encrypted form. Anyone with the CD-ROM can typically test drive the software sample a few times. To purchase and take delivery of a given product, you call an 800 number and issue a credit card number in exchange for the code to unlock the selected software. Electronic documentation is usually included, but the hard copy is also usually shipped within a few days.

Software encryption facilitates "try before you buy"

14

Information Management

The technologies associated with multimedia bring new power to business computing in general. CD-ROM, graphics, audio, and video all have powerful uses when integrated with traditional business vehicles such as publishing and databases. While some of these applications stretch the meaning of the term "multimedia," they are nonetheless viable business solutions.

Multimedia is merging with traditional business applications

Audio-Visual Databases

Databases have proven to be invaluable at cataloging and retrieving vast amounts of information. More and more database products can now incorporate media such as graphics, sound, and video in addition to text. Perhaps the most obvious application is keeping track of media elements for production purposes. The ability to search for media elements according to specific criteria really comes into play as production resources grow and different people are handling production responsibilities. On a larger scale, film and video producers can audition talent from audio-visual screen tests. Theaters and studios can choose and locate props from warehouses and backlots. Ad agencies can keep track of collateral, commercials, and ad campaigns for various clients.

Multimedia databases can aid the production process

On a broader base, multimedia databases can be used to keep track of business commodities. In large corporations, employee databases are being used for security and human resources, as well as matching employee attributes with teams and tasks. Service and tech support departments can benefit by viewing procedures by example. Doctors can locate and view x-rays and unusual medical procedures instantly in both normal and emergency situations. Government agencies can search, compare, and transmit fingerprints and photos. Some segments of the real-estate industry are employing virtual MLS (multiple listing service) to streamline the process of matching properties with buyers—especially over long distances in the case of corporate relocations. The travel industry can use multimedia to

Multimedia databases can also track many types of commodities

help clients visualize destinations and plan trips. In general, any commodity with a vast number of options and searchable criteria is a candidate for multimedia databasing.

Electronic Publishing

Electronic publishing adds value at potentially lower costs

The storage capacity, size, weight, and price of CD-ROMs provide a compelling publishing alternative to paper. The real key here is adding value by offering more than the print version. Low-cost color and fewer cost restrictions can facilitate expanded coverage. Audio, video, and animation can also add a tremendous amount of richness to coverage in everything from interviews to tutorials to point-of-interest stories. Interactivity can help individuals locate topics of interest more quickly—and *hypertext* offers the ability to explore topics from various angles and with greater depth. (Hypertext is most commonly thought of as clicking on a word to bring up definitions or navigate to other iterations and contexts.)

Catalogs are prime candidates for electronic publishing

Many manufacturers with large product lines or parts catalogs are embracing CD-ROM as a vehicle for supplying business partners with catalogs. With or without full use of multimedia, the ability to search electronically for requested information and the cost difference between producing and mailing CD-ROMs versus catalogs the size of telephone books is extremely compelling.

CD-ROM makes it possible to produce virtual press kits

Ad agencies and corporate communications departments are also examining CD-ROM publishing as supplements to print. CD-ROMs can contain the text of press releases and white papers, reviewer's guides, virtual brochures, promotional videos, and high-resolution photographs, logos, and line art that may all be useful to publications, clients, and business partners. Moreover, the capacity of CD-ROMs makes it possible to centralize all current information about a client or product line on a single disc.

Electronic publishing as discussed here primarily refers to usage for business communication. Many traditional publishers are now examining, if not pursuing, electronic publishing. The multimedia wave is also producing a sort of feeding frenzy where anybody with content (or even an idea for content) is looking into CD-ROM publishing. While this book is about the use of multimedia in business rather than the business of multimedia, a few words are in order here. First, the electronic version should be more compelling than print and more than a little attention must be given to aesthetics. Second, the installed base of multimedia computers is still very small when compared to that of people who can read the printed word. Finally, the marketing channels for multimedia titles are still being established. Stores respectively carrying books, videos, and software are often interested in CD-ROM titles yet unwilling to take much of a risk at this writing. Until the paving of the information superhighway, creative specialty marketing is often required to make electronic publishing a profitable venture.

Electronic publishing for the mass market is only in the beginning stages

Information on Demand

In the Information Age, pure information is a salable commodity that often blurs the lines between product and service. On-line services currently represent a business model based on information on demand. Businesses take advantage of these services because specific research on a vast amount of subjects can be performed in a short period of time. While a premium is charged for research of more specialized topics, the adage of time equaling money evens things out. Usage of electronics for data acquisition will continue to proliferate as more content is available on-line, more people use these services, and modem speeds increase. While the expansion of Internet is currently fueling the fire, limitations in transmission speeds are still placing an emphasis on text. The bandwidth and accessibility of the information superhighway stands to blow the lid off this industry since its bandwidth facilitates volumes of content that are much more media rich.

Information on demand is an increasingly viable service business

High-speed modems are opening interesting doors without waiting for the information superhighway to be paved. A prime example is the availability of stock photography catalogs on line from companies like Kodak. Art directors can log onto a vast virtual catalog via modem, enter search

Virtual catalogs serving business are already available on-line

criteria for the type of photo needed, download small thumbnails of the qualifying images for browsing, possibly download a larger version of a prime candidate for comping purposes, then order the high-res version to be delivered via overnight services. Such services typically incur a subscription fee, possible charges for on-line time, and respectable purchase prices for the final product.

High-speed cable modems may also facilitate information services such as Internet at speeds of around 3MBps via cable TV long before fiber optic and set-top players are ubiquitous.

15

Business Communications

Electronics have continually changed the way businesses communicate, from the advent of the telephone through radio, television, fax, computers, modems, and cellular technologies. While the term "multimedia" is most commonly used to describe a closed system such as a computer with a CD-ROM, that model is expanding to networking. Moreover, parallel advances in communications technologies are rapidly expanding the model and blurring the lines between the two industries. The digital realm makes it relatively simple to combine, transmit, and receive data representing various combinations of information and media. While in-depth coverage of the myriad communications technologies merging with multimedia is beyond the scope of this book, here's a quick look at major trends.

Multimedia is a natural evolution of communication technologies

V-Mail

Voice mail and E-mail have become ubiquitous in businesses everywhere. Their popularity owes in no small degree to the fact that they allow busy people to communicate effectively using a sort of time-shifting metaphor, circumventing much of the phone tag associated with leaving brief messages with secretaries and other associates. The proliferation of multimedia computing brings the logical evolution of V-mail—electronic mail utilizing video.

Video mail is a logical extension of voice mail and E-mail

V-mail has several benefits. First, it adds a human factor by allowing recipients to see the sender. Second, V-mail also facilitates pointing the camera at physical objects such as models and comps. Finally, dedicated V-mail will become sophisticated enough to incorporate documents of many different data types—video, animation, spreadsheets, charts, letters, faxes, and so forth—into a single communication.

Proper use of V-mail can improve productivity

V-mail can take two forms. The ultimate incarnation will use video servers and isochronous multimedia networking protocols to deliver video in real time. Operating much like the client-server technology found in

V-mail software holds the key to effectiveness

E-mail and voice mail, this reduces the storage burden on the part of the individual workstations. While this technology exists today, it is far from entrenched. It also requires V-mail software at all participating workstations. Such software would typically allow a single message to contain video, text, and other business documents.

E-mailing digital video files is a short-term alternative

The other solution is the creation of digital videos that are transmitted as attached documents to everyday E-mail. A large volume of these documents can burden the storage capacity of the server and throughput of a traditional network. Without integrated V-mail software, a video file would take the form of a standard QuickTime or AVI movie produced using normal digital video editing software and would be viewed using a standard player. Other related documents such as text and spreadsheets would be viewed in their respective applications. Very few people are embracing this awkward method, waiting instead for mainstream V-mail.

Acceptance of V-mail will come with other communication advances

Any form of video mail requires one other component—a camera on the transmitting end. While desktop communication cameras are becoming available at reasonable prices, the expense of upgrading an entire system with cameras and V-mail software at each station, along with video servers and multimedia-compliant networks is questionable today in light of the benefits. It's sort of like putting in a telephone system for the primary reason that it will bring voice mail—rather than the fact that people need to use telephones! V-mail will most likely only really take off when the information superhighway enables visual communication on a more common level.

Videoconferencing

Videoconferencing is most effective when contrasted with travel expense

In its simplest form, videoconferencing can be thought of as a two-way, closed-circuit television hookup where both parties can see and hear the other. The model can be expanded to that of a conference call between multiple sites, and to include transmission of electronic documents. Sometimes known as "telepresencing," videoconferencing can provide a cost-effective alternative to flying to meetings—especially when the travel expenses and down time of several colleagues are involved. The technology really starting being put to use during the Gulf War when international travel was of questionable safety.

Currently, videoconferencing to remote locations requires expensive technology dedicated to two-way narrowcasts. This will soon give way to full-duplex solutions similar to two-way phone conversations on a single line. The associated cost is often prohibitive for all but the largest corporations, spawning videoconferencing sites that can be rented on a per-session basis in various cities. The use of dedicated lines or satellites to facilitate these transmissions can still make videoconferencing quite costly even without the actual hardware investment. Although there is nonetheless a high satisfaction rating, we should see significant improvements in audio-graphic point-to-point and multilocation conferencing over the next year.

Videoconferencing is still expensive

Videoconferencing is currently less costly to implement within organizations that have high-speed LANs and WANs, since they don't need to address the issue of site-to-site communications. These networks must be upgraded to multimedia standards with isochronous protocols and video servers, as well as cameras and other ancillary equipment at each location. Currently, the cost-effectiveness within an organization with a single office building or even campus is questionable since actual meetings can be scheduled with reasonable ease. The investment currently makes more sense for companies with several sites separated by significant distances.

Internal videoconferencing requires multimedia network capabilities

Videoconferencing also has a relationship with the *collaborative computing* model taking shape on the business horizon. The basic concept is that users at several different stations can be working on the same document while talking simultaneously via phone. Some venders are offering software enablers that transmit both voice and data over the same phone line. While this is a step in the right direction, the addition of real-time video ups the ante significantly past the capabilities of normal phone lines.

Collaborative computing will integrate with videoconferencing

As with V-mail, videoconferencing will probably not see widespread use until the infrastructure of the information superhighway matures. At that point, the novelty of videoconferencing will simply transform into the way in which people communicate, much as they use telephones today.

Videoconferencing will be commonplace

16

Future Directions

Given the rate at which multimedia technology and applications are evolving, it's very appropriate to wrap things up with a look at where it's all going. Multimedia is destined to evolve beyond a phenomenon into part of the overall fabric of modern society. Much of it is interwoven with the overall momentum of the Information Age.

Multimedia will become part of mainstream media

Ubiquitous Multimedia

Anyone who has tracked technology for any length of time knows that there's no stopping the wheels of progress. Multimedia technology will continue to offer more power in smaller packages for lower prices. It is predicted that within a few short years, all computers will be multimedia capable. Audio, video, interactivity, and other multimedia elements will become so ingrained in computing culture that the concept of multimedia is likely to become one and the same with generic computing. Multimedia computing will simply be everywhere.

All computing will be multimedia computing

The same miniaturization that has stuffed the power of last decade's mainframes into laptops and VCR/TV technology into Watchmans will make multimedia more portable. Color active matrix LCD screens are getting larger, lighter, and less expensive. Advances in battery technology are expected to extend battery life—and with it, the practicality of remote multimedia. The continued evolution of cellular communications will also make it possible to exchange multimedia content with central locations from remote locations.

Miniaturization and cellular technology will make multimedia more portable

Multimedia is also destined to become less isolated on individual computers and grow into a collaborative computing phenomenon. As the uses for multimedia proliferate and acceptance grows, networks will gradually take on the hardware and software capabilities required for enterprise multimedia. Initially, compromises will be made on existing copper wire, but the paving of the information superhighway will eventually bring a fiber-optic

Networked multimedia will be commonplace

infrastructure to most businesses that will facilitate full-blown networked multimedia tied seamlessly into everyday business communication technologies like phone, fax, and E-mail. Indeed, these services as well as videoconferencing and V-mail are likely to meld into a single system that serves all business communication needs.

The Information Superhighway

The information superhighway will integrate many forms of communication

Much of the excitement on the multimedia horizon surrounds the advent of the information superhighway—essentially the vision of all homes and businesses interconnected in an interactive audio-visual-data network. This infrastructure is touted as being the seamless integration of all communication services including television, telephone, fax, modem, E-mail, home entertainment, and more. Many visionaries see the total implementation of this technology as the realization of a virtual community where communication, services, business, consumer, and social activities can be conducted across town or around the world with similar ease.

Technology Overview

Tremendous bandwidth is required

From a technology standpoint, the race is being fueled by digital media. As described in Chapter 2, any media in digital form can be transmitted by the same type of conduit without regard to content. Thanks to compression technology, modest services can be carried via the copper wire used by some telephone and cable companies. The sheer amount of data required to carry the full palette of two-way, real-time services expected ultimately demands the entrenchment of fiber-optic cable. This type of conduit can carry roughly 25,000 times the amount of information as its copper counterpart. Moreover, fiber cable is often laid in bundles of 48 separate conduits, each with this same formidable bandwidth.

Compression is still necessary

The amount of services offered and the number of customers requiring services still requires compression technology. A variety of compression technologies optimized for various media and applications will complement each other in providing a spectrum of services. In particular, MPEG 2 is the compression method emerging for content such as motion picture and television transmission.

The first form of this new infrastructure is being touted as 500 channels, largely because it is a concept that most people can easily grasp. In actuality, the concept of dedicated channels will disappear. Program content such as movies and home shopping will be stored in large computers masquerading as cable stations. When these services are selected for viewing, a series of data packets representing the content will be sent down the fiber bearing IDs for their various destinations. Intelligent hardware incorporating audio-visual computing technology on the receiving end will pick up the appropriate packets and decipher them for presentation. In short, the concept of the information superhighway is really that of the ultimate wide-area, wide-band network.

The information superhighway will really be a large computer network

Some experts see the existing Internet structure as that upon which the information superhighway can be built. Internet already has two-way communication over standard phone lines, established communication and addressing protocols, and a sea of global information providers. On the down side, it is currently based on the rather arcane UNIX protocol and is primarily used for real-time transfer of text and nonreal-time transfer of other digital media. In order for Internet to be of practical widespread use, effective advances need to include a friendly, graphically oriented user interface and fiber-optic conduits.

Internet is one possibility

Regardless of the physical form taken by the information superhighway, selection and navigation of the vast area of services is a formidable challenge. The number of virtual channels and subscription costs render the modern practice of channel surfing impractical. Viewing guides the size of telephone books are certainly no more practical. On-line versions of such directories must have formidable search capabilities. One possible solution is that of a personal electronic agent programmed to understand your interests and viewing desires. This model eliminates some of the chance and whimsy associated with personal choice. Another solution is that of subscribing to an information broker who offers a palette of viewing selections that you choose from, much in the way that we select certain newspapers, magazines, premium channels, and movie critics—for their taste and style.

Navigation is a major issue

Implementation

Bandwidth throughout the system is the key technology issue

The difficulty in implementing this digital infrastructure lies primarily in the fact that the digital information system must reach every home or business that wishes to participate, just as a highway system needs on- and off-ramps for access. And, like a traditional highway, the throughput is only as efficient as that of the smallest artery. Data carried by fiber-optic cable across the country or across town will bottleneck if it hits copper cable on your street. Moreover, the compression needed for real-time, two-way video requires fiber in order to move past the handful of frames-per-second and miniature images exhibited in today's picture phones.

The market is highly competitive

The federal government's deregulation of the communications industry now has traditional information providers scrambling to be *the* information provider. Telephone and cable companies are on the front lines of the battle for your living room since they have the two most entrenched conduits into homes and businesses. We've all seen the propaganda bandied about by leaders in these industries positioning themselves in the public's collective consciousness as the source of all future information. Other traditional media providers such as broadcast networks, movie studios, record companies, and print publishers are also assessing how they fit into this new communication model.

Cable and telephone providers will likely share the implementation

The cable industry is established in the public eye as providers of one-way audio-visual entertainment to our living rooms. Conversely, the telephone companies have developed a two-way communication network that spans the globe with voice and data—and with a better reputation for service. The recent scramble for alliances between major players in these two camps is indicative of the reluctance on either side to risk losing it all to the other. Some experts feel that the significantly better funding and entrenchment enjoyed by the telephone companies may ultimately unseat the cable industry altogether as information services combine.

Smart information appliances are required as well

Consumer electronics and computer manufacturers are also taking part in the race. Ultimately, smart appliances will need to navigate, record, and transmit information across the communications infrastructure—both in businesses and homes. While these two industries have been embracing multimedia technology, the difficulty is that many home computers and entertainment players are isolated from the communications universe.

Moreover, computers are rarely found in the living room or entertainment center, and audio-visual technology has barely scratched the surface of everyday business computing. As a result, manufacturers are scrambling to produce consumer devices that integrate directly into home entertainment centers and don't look and feel like computers. Similarly, multimedia technology is being increasingly woven into traditional computers and networks.

Set-top players such as 3DO and CD-I are basically computers clothed as home entertainment devices. While this technology has been slow to gain mass acceptance, we are likely to see rapid evolution in the next few years. One factor is that these devices will grow to facilitate the intelligence required for navigation of the information superhighway and storage of received data. Another driving force is likely to be a push to Video CD on the part of the video rental industry before the widespread interconnection of all homes and businesses. Unlike videotape, Video CDs don't wear out after a few dozen rentals and are less susceptible to physical wear and heat abuse. We are likely to see a parallel to the music industry where LPs were hard to come by once CD players reached critical mass. Simultaneously, the cost of recordable CD-ROM technology is anticipated to plummet to the point where it will replace the VCR for most uses.

Set-top players are likely to replace VCRs

Impact

The advent of the information superhighway will impact consumers in a variety of ways. Obviously, the viewing options will make today's cable systems pale by comparison—at least with regard to quantity. As for quality, there will be a plethora of home shopping channels, direct marketing channels, TV reruns, and movie libraries. Viewer selection of viewing time represents the ultimate in time shifting. Two-way audio-visual communication will also improve person-to-person and consumer-to-business communications. One of the gray areas is who will foot the bill for all of this new technology.

Consumers will gain many more content options

While the information superhighway will impact consumers on a wide range of other levels, our main concern here is the impact on business. The most obvious are in business-to-business communications. Videophone-style communications will add a great deal of personalization to business calls. Much of the time consumed by traveling to business

Everyday business-to-business communication will improve

meetings can be obviated when live presentations can be delivered remotely, complete with support from data and audio-visual aids. Personnel in the field can be much more integrated into the everyday internal communications of their companies. Much of the material that is currently delivered via overnight services will also be accommodated on-line due to increased throughput and standard protocols.

Business-to-consumer communication will be more direct

The other major area in which business will benefit is in business-to-consumer communications. Any company with a direct marketing need can benefit from consumer access to this communications infrastructure. Interactive audio-visual Yellow Pages will provide an initial method by which businesses can distinguish their products and services. Moreover, given the model of a mammoth wide-area network, any business can become an information provider with its own virtual channel—complete with home shopping. In short, the communication between businesses and consumers will be encouraged to become much more open and direct.

The information superhighway will impact business as significantly as has the computer

The full implementation of the information superhighway is unclear. Like our paved highway system, it will likely be a combination of interconnected conduits provided by various service providers. The bottom line is that it will be only as good as the weakest link in any given communication path. It will also be several years before we see the promise of this technology really begin to take effect. It is more realistic to expect the interconnection of all businesses and households in approximately 10 to 15 years. Just as the face of entertainment, communication, and business has changed dramatically in the past 15 years, it is impossible to foresee the complete impact of the information superhighway combined with multimedia technology—both from a technological and cultural standpoint. It is nonetheless clear that this combination of technologies is likely to revolutionize business as dramatically as the computer has in the brief period since its inception.

Index